FEMININE PROGRESSION
How I Walked Out of Masculinity

BY
SOPHIA RUFFIN

LIFE TO LEGACY

Feminine Progression:
How I walked Out of Masculinity
Sophia Ruffin, Copyright ©2017

ISBN-13: 978-1-947288-06-5
ISBN-10: 1-947288-06-7

Scripture quotations are taken from the Authorized King James Version.

Printed in the United States
10 9 8 7 6 5 4 3 2 1

Cover design by: Traneisha Y. Jones

Published by
Life To Legacy, LLC
P.O. Box 1239
Matteson, IL 60443
877-267-7477
www.Life2Legacy.com
Life2legacybooks@att.net

PRESENTED TO:

Contents

DEDICATION

I would like to take the time to give thanks, glory and honor to God who has been my solid rock; and who has been faithful to watch over His word to perform it in my life. I am forever grateful for the processes I experienced, which has given me the endurance to continue to progress.

To my beautiful mother who has been my friend, thank you for never leaving or forsaking me. Thank you for protecting and covering me in prayer, and never giving up on me. I love you and I am so happy you are alive to witness the transformation in my life. Daddy, thank you for being such a powerful, amazing, and loving father. I absolutely love you and appreciate you for being a demonstration of growth, and being the difference maker for your bloodline. I witnessed you progress in so many areas, and as God did it for you, He was faithful to do it for me.

Grandma Base, I love you and I am so blessed God has allowed you to see that your prayers were not in vain. Thank you for being a praying grandmother. Your mantle was passed down, and I am grateful for being able to carry it. I will always seek to make you smile. To my Uncle Lorenzo, you have always been one of my number one fans, and you still are. You have been like a second father who shows love and support daily, thank you. To all of my aunts and uncles, thank you.

To my siblings Alison, Lindsey, and Reggie thanks for the support, prayers, and love. I am so blessed to have each of you. Alison, thank you for being an incredible sister and for being a part of my progression. You have always told me to be myself, all while praying and helping me grow into the woman I am today, both naturally and spiritually. You prophesied this and more, thank you.

Devon, thank you for being an awesome friend. You have been endless through this journey and have assisted in helping me overcome barriers. You have allowed God to use you to be a friend who went through the fire, to pull me out of the pit. I can go on and on, but we will let the readers see just how special you are as they continue to read.

Apostle Tim and Kelley Brinson, thank you for being the amazing jewels used to catapult me from darkness into light. I appreciate your ministry, and truly know you shall be blessed all the days of your life for your faithfulness.

Apostle John Eckhart, #COACH, thank you for believing in me and giving me the opportunities of a lifetime. I thank God for you every day, and can't believe God has given me favor with you. Your book, *Prayers that Deroute Demons*, played a critical role in my deliverance and helped me along the journey of my life. I am in awe of God and how He used you at the beginning of my journey through a book, and He is using you now to stretch, advance, and progress me into new dimensions of His power. Coach, I love you and thank God for you. You are a blessing to me and I have received multiple impartations from you through your books, witnessing you minister, and being in your presence. Know that who you are to the kingdom is great, and you will be a voice in the earth forever.

FOREWORD

There are multitudes of people who are struggling with their identity. This is especially true in the area of sexuality. This is a sensitive area for many, and some people react strongly against anyone who dares imply that people can or should change. Sophia Ruffin challenges some teaching that is prevalent today, and does it in love as she gives her testimony to back up what she believes and knows.

Sophia Ruffin's testimony will challenge and stir you. This book will give hope to the hopeless, and encourage anyone struggling with their identity to become an overcomer. This is not just another book on the subject of sexuality. It contains truth that will set anyone free. I am amazed at how God is using Sophia and her journey to bring deliverance to multitudes. The Lord is using her writings to reach people that she may never personally meet. However, by reading this book, you will feel as if you know her. She is open and not afraid to tell her story without shame.

Some have been taught that you cannot change who you are when it comes to your sexuality. Some have believed that they are destined to be a certain way. God wants us to know the truth. Deliverance and transformation are real. Many have experienced it. Some have written about it, and others have testified. Sophia is adding to the increasing volume of voices that testify of God's grace and mercy.

This book will take you into the heart of the subject of feminism and the struggle for some to move into it. This is not an easy journey. The difficulties and challenges one may encounter will be expressed in this book, but there is hope. There is nothing impossible with God. God's power is available to all. God's mercy is great, and His patience is overwhelming.

This book will also help the church to minister properly to people who are struggling in this area. We need compassion and understanding to minister to people of all backgrounds. At times, the church has failed in this area. However, we cannot hide from this subject. We must be able to relate to one of the major issues of our day. We cannot afford to be ignorant of one of the greatest challenges of our generation. This book will help us rise up to meet the challenge.

Be blessed as you read the pages of this book. Let Sophia's story bless, encourage, and if needed, deliver you. The truth will set you free. Let the truth of this book liberate you from anything that is holding you back, and preventing you from being all that God desire for you to be.

—John Eckhardt
Crusaders Church
Founder of I.M.P.A.C.T. Network
Best-selling Author of *Prayers That Route Demons*

Introduction

As I sat in my living room having a conversation with Godly counselors, I found my heart open and ready to take the initial step towards giving my life to God. The words pierced my heart, so I scooted towards the edge of my seat with my mouth wide open as I took in every word. With my eyes widened, my nose dripping in sweat, and my heart pounding, I lifted my hands in surrender. For a moment I drifted from who I was to who I could become. I lost track of the battles I was facing and wanted to drift into this new found love that was being articulated so wonderfully. Tears that were dried up and ancient rose from a depth of which I had forgotten. Like an ocean ready to release a wave, halted, as I heard these words, "Sophia, I would love for you to visit my church, however, before you come, you will need to put on a skirt." Stunned, shocked, and humiliated my eyes shut, my head dropped, and my heart sunk in great disappointment. At that very moment, the door to my heart shut abruptly, and I put a code around it vowing to keep it locked. I then thought to myself, "Skirt? A skirt? I don't even own a skirt, what in the world are you thinking? Can't you look at me and tell I'm a man, and men don't wear skirts. Therefore, thanks but no thanks."

Three years after that conversation, I refused to entertain the idea of showing my face in anybody's church service. After that encounter, I had many people to approach me saying, "Sophia come visit my church. You will enjoy our church because you are able to come as you are." I would immediately respond with, "Are people like me welcome," while giving them the side eye. They would express, "Come as you are Sophia, God accepts you just the way you are." I would give myself the stare down, and wonder if the church was really ready to embrace a lesbian stud. Would they stare at me? Would they judge me? Would they make me change my clothes? Would I have to put on a dress? I didn't mind changing my life or even changing my heart but giving up my clothes and the way I dressed was out of the equation. It wasn't even an option. I wasn't willing to compromise or consider the idea. I would hear over and over, "Sophia God weighs the matters of the heart. God knows your heart, come on and visit my church." And the answer would always end with a bold proclamation, "Nope!"

Telling me that God knew my heart wasn't a punch line that swayed me forward. To be honest, those very words scared me to death and pushed me backward. The fact that God knows my heart brought forth a terrible fear because my heart was so far from God. If my heart were to be judged by a Holy King, no doubt, I would be found guilty. The weight was heavy, and I was clueless about what it all meant, so it was easier to deny the invitation, rather than accept it. I preferred to perish for lack of knowledge, rather than to know

God and to refuse to obey.

The most amazing part of my journey was how these same people who said I could come as I was were the same people who shamed me when I walked inside the church with a heart of a woman, but the appearance of a man. I struggled for years, trying to comprehend God, due to Him being misrepresented by the church. I was bound in gross darkness in search of light, and I was looking for someone to be that beacon who could direct me to the God I heard about, and the God I read about. I was being killed between the porch and the altar in search of the Savior. When man couldn't get past my natural presentation, God captured me by my spiritual desperation and called me to Himself.

I am so grateful that when man failed to lead me to the altar, God came to my rescue, and drew me with His light and His love. The power of God rolled out the red carpet in the spirit realm, and escorted me into His presence, giving me access to speak with Him mouth-to-mouth and face to face.

Now roll up your sleeves, open the eyes of your heart, and join me on my journey as I take you behind the scenes into some of the most broken seasons of my life.

I am so blessed to have the opportunity to write this book and bring you through the process of my experiences post altar, by sharing my step-by-step transformation. I am writing this book because there are many people who have alternative lifestyles and struggle to receive Jesus because of a misrepresentation of the church. I want to use my personal story of progression, and how God progressively walked me out of sin into wholeness, with the intent to shatter the power of darkness that was keeping me from embracing the fullness of His presence. This journey wasn't easy, it was a death walk, and I found myself carrying my cross daily. Although the process was painful, I stood on the Word of God that declares, "I would never leave you or forsake you, Sophia. I will give you double honor for your shame, and I will give you beauty for ashes in the days to come."

I pray that this book ministers to the core of your heart. I also pray that you would read it with an open heart, and allow my experience to be a blueprint to help you in your process. Whether you are a leader, a parent, or a person bound by sin, this book will truly bless you, not because I wrote it, but because I lived it, so that you could be freed.

Disclaimer: I am not saying that putting on feminine attire proves your deliverance. I am declaring that God has the power to RESET your life by restoring your identity to its original state. I am not writing this book to condemn you or make you feel you are not saved because of your exterior. I am writing to encourage you that HE that began a good work in your life will complete it. You may never change your attire, and you may never go through the phases I went through, but you will be transformed into the image God has ordained for you. May *Feminine Progression* be a blessing to you.

One

After the Altar, Now What?

COME AS YOU ARE HUH? SO Y'ALL GONNA KEEP TELLING me I can come to church the way I am. I remember the last time I considered attending church, the first thing I was told was to put on a skirt, and that didn't go over so well. I refused to be dirty on the inside but clean on the outside. I wanted my cup cleaned inside-out. So after a few years of convincing, I thought over and over about giving God a try. I really wanted to be in church, and I desired to know God, but it was so hard to reach Him when so many of His leaders were acting as His security in the earth. They were refusing to grant people access into His presence if they didn't look, sound, or dress according to the church's standard of holiness. Heck, I was far from Holy. I was a sinner in need of a Savior. Each time I attempted to go into the house of God, I was mocked, condemned and shamed. I would suddenly become the sermon topic, God didn't make Adam and Steve and was rejected based on my appearance. I would think to myself, "Did Jesus come to save the sinner or the saint, because I'm confused on who's being called to salvation." I needed to drink from the well, but the well was highly guarded by men and women of God putting on a form of Godliness but denying the power. I would run out of church, stating over and over, "I guess if God wants me, He's going to have to come get me Himself."

And Then This Happened

One hot Sunday morning in 2003 that's exactly what happened. God used my sense of humor to lure me to service. I was planning on attending church to prank a friend who was desperately pulling on me to visit her church. I laughed at the idea and asked myself how many epic failures did I need to experience before proving that people like me weren't accepted in church. However, on this particular Sunday, something on the inside kept saying, "Sophia just go, just give this church a try, and get a good laugh out of it." I actually laughed out loud at the idea and thought to give it a go. On top of good humor, I heard good things about this particular ministry, so that was enough to push me to enter the four walls of the church. Before attending, I didn't try to fix myself up to fit the quote unquote protocol of the church. I came just the way I was. I walked into service with my sexuality, masculinity, and the very sin that many declared would send me straight to hell. I was unashamed and confident in who I was.

I was super curious about attending service as I got dressed. I called a homie to roll with me, and prepared to make my way downtown for church. Deep down, there was something on the inside that was anticipating something unusual, yet I couldn't put my finger on it. I mean, I grew up in a Baptist church as a child. I thought I knew God, and I was convinced I was saved, I just wasn't living the Word. As a kid, and even a teenager, I was always going to the altar to be born again. I can recall sitting in church as a kid, hearing convicting messages, and always having this feeling that I wasn't saved. I learned the fear of the Lord early in life, yet my rebellion was so strong, it was like unto witchcraft causing me to reject the very God I needed for salvation. One thing I learned is when God has a plan for your life, and a timing on your destiny, it can't be altered or reversed, so the thing I called curiosity, was really God drawing me. God was in it, and I couldn't outrun His timing. So me attending church service in '03 out of curiosity and a joke, turned out to be the day destiny met purpose, and it was already scheduled and ordained in the heavens. God just used the moment of what I called a joke, to become the moment I would encounter Him, and the day everything changed.

Well Here It Goes

You know you saved for real, for real, in real life when you can remember the specifics of your salvation like it was yesterday. I can recall the conversations I had with myself before walking into church.

I rolled up to the spot where they say, "the anointing goes down." I was ready to find out but first, let me get myself together. In the parking lot, I looked around suspiciously, yet anxiously awaiting what was ahead. As I took off my black do-rag, I checked to make sure my waves were intact. I had the 360 deep ocean waves, so I grabbed my hard wooden brush, pulled down the sun visor and began to brush until the waves were spinning like the Pacific Ocean. I reached into my pocket, grabbed my chap stick, rubbed it on my lips, brushed my fade a little more, and said, "Let's do this Sophia." "Do what," I thought to myself. I'm not exactly sure what I was planning on doing, but Lord knows, He sure had a plan that day. I jumped out of my tan Chevy Impala, told my homie to come on, and we walked inside the church. I attempted to pull up my pants, licked my finger to wipe the dust off my brown Doc Martin Shoes, and headed inside the old movie theater, which had been refurbished into a church. I approached the door, and my heart pounded as I walked in to find my seat. I looked around, and I could see people looking and anticipating a great day of taking me down. Although that may not have been their thoughts, I sure felt like they were ready for a day of great deliverance.

Ushers were on their post, the praise team was singing, and people were standing, dancing, leaping and shouting. I walked in feeling so cool, so chilled, and so nervous. I was happy to be there because I could now tell people I had done a good deed and actually attended church. To my surprise, no one looked at me weird or made me feel like a freak. Yet I thought to myself, "Sophia whatever you do, don't allow these people to get to you." I was determined to chill and enjoy church, without getting caught up in the emotions of it all. I shifted my focus off the people, as I looked for a seat, and focused on keeping my swag together because my image was everything to me, and this was a joke. The fact that Sophia Ruffin was in service, sitting down, and complying with the flow, was major.

Here I am looking around, and ready to quickly find me a seat. I walked to the upper level, popped my feet up in the seat in front of me, and watched service and the time on my watch as I thought to myself, "I'm out of here at 1:00. Regardless if they are done or not, they have until 1:00 p.m. Service was going forth, and after a few minutes in, I began to feel out of place. I was getting uncomfortable in my own skin and didn't know what was going on. All my chill and swag was beginning to fail me. I kept trying to fix my mannerisms and countenance because I couldn't expose my weakness. As I gazed around the building, there wasn't a soul in there to whom I could relate. I was the only one in the church that was a stud, and with the community being extremely small, I had no privacy. I felt like all eyes were on me. I'm not sure if they were staring, but I know the entire service, all types of weird things were happening that made me more and more uncomfortable. I tried to put my hands between my legs, I tried to slouch in my seat, and if I could have gotten away with it, I would have sat Indian style.

People were shouting, jumping, speaking in unknown tongues, and getting their church on. While I sat cool, observing everyone with a sarcastic smirk on my face, and saying to myself, "When this is over? I will never return." There wasn't anything wrong with the church; there was something wrong with me. As the service continued, the Man of God walked in, sat in the front row, and prepared to grab the mic to minister. My eyes got big as I recalled meeting this man in the barber shop a few weeks prior and being freaked out because his presence provoked my demons to tremble. Every time I would see this man, I would shake, and wonder what's up with this dude. His anointing was destroying yokes in my life without my consent. As he preached, I was in awe of the power in which he spoke, and how powerfully he delivered his message. I was captivated by his ability to speak about Jesus and the love of God with power, compassion, and conviction. As he completed his sermon, he requested for everyone to stand on their feet. For some odd reason, I felt like my knees had locked, because I was unable to move. I looked around, held my neighbor's hand, and continued to sit. I literally couldn't stand on my feet. It looked as if I was being rebellious. However, it felt like there was a weight on my body that wouldn't allow me to move.

The praise team began to sing Martha Munizzi's *God Is Here.* The song reverberated in my soul as the words, "He is here to break the yoke and lift the heavy burden," penetrated my heart. That phrase seemed to increase in volume and intensity. Something was happening that I couldn't explain. I was beginning to believe God was actually present, and that He was calling me. Regardless, I had no intentions on surrendering my life to God; besides, I loved my life. I sure wasn't prepared to give it away. I didn't want to share my life with God, and I sure wasn't ready for the level of commitment needed to live a life of purity and holiness. Holiness wasn't even in my vocabulary. I couldn't help but wonder what in the world could God do with me. I'm way too far out there for God to desire me. I was convinced that I was too far from God to be found, and if God came near me my only place of eternity was total damnation to hell. It felt like life was paused and I wondered what in the world God could do with my life. I kept saying, "I'm gay. I'm happy with my life. I look like a man. I am displeasing to God. God is angry with me, how could He desire me.

Something awkward was happening the more the praise team sang, the more I felt the sting of death gripping my body and taking my breath away. Let's just say I died that day. God took my breath away, apprehended me and escorted me to the altar. My jersey number in the spirit realm was called and God was prepared to put me in the game. I was preparing to join Team Jesus, and I hadn't even tried out. I was being summoned by the host of heaven without my consent. The weight of the invitation was heavy, and who could resist such power when it comes with strength, might and authority. As I stood up to walk the green mile from my seat to the altar, I could hear the voice of God with so much clarity.

I hesitated and had a difficult time making my way to the altar. I knew there was more to it than going to the altar and quoting the sinners prayer. To me, it felt like I was preparing to memorialize my flesh, give my life up, and be deployed into the kingdom of God. I didn't know what all that meant, but I knew there was more to it than just saying a prayer. I was walking into a covenant commitment that I was preparing to embrace. I didn't comprehend the details of it all, but if God chose me, I was sure He had the answers. To the altar, I went as I heard the voice of God promising to protect me, and to make good on His Word. I was completely handled with care by the Holy Spirit, and for the first time in my life, I trusted a presence I couldn't see.

You may ask how did I know it was the voice of God speaking. I knew it was a power higher than me, a God who had total authority, dominion and power to grip my soul, and carry me to the altar. It was a gentle yet firm voice of a Father that affirmed my existence in the earth; a voice of love and security, and a voice that I recognized as God, my God. The voice of the Lord was strong, powerful, and like the sound of a Father awaiting His child with open arms. It was a voice I couldn't deny, and a voice that was like none other. As tears streamed down my cheeks, heartbroken and bowed heart before the Lord. I was ready to say yes. Yes to whatever the request would be. At this moment I was vulnerable and open to receive. The voice of God took authority over the conversations in my head. At that moment I blanked out and zoned in on Him, recklessly abandoning myself to bow to the voice that makes heaven and earth stand still. I couldn't comprehend why God was calling me to the altar or why God was speaking to me. I simply embraced the moment. I seized it for what it was.

Then the Lord declared, "Daughter I chose you, you didn't choose me. I chose you before the foundations of the world. And again He declared, "It is I. I chose you Sophia." I could feel the tangibility of God. The Word of the Lord continued to speak as I continued to make my way to the altar. He declared, "Before I wrapped you in flesh and sent you forth in the earth, I had a plan for your life. I know your end before your beginning. I'm going to use you daughter. I have plans for your life." The tears erupted like a volcano releasing lava all over the place. At that moment destiny kissed purpose. I was wrecked, undone, and a total mess. I forgot about my life and was driven to the power that evoked the very strands of my hair to stand. Oh how strong, secure, and confident God was as He Spoke life to my feeble soul.

As I made it to the altar, the voice shifted, and suddenly the man standing before me began to speak. I was able to decipher between the two voices, and at this point, I was open to receive. The Man of God spoke prophetically into my life. He removed the microphone and spoke my childhood with clarity and accuracy. He described my experiences and declared the same words God had just spoken to me. Chills went down my spine as I stood frozen yet astonished by this powerful experience of heaven and earth coming together to fulfill my God-given destiny. I immediately thrusted after the God who revealed my secrets to such a man. The fact that God shared my secrets with this man, and how the man of God handled me with care, I was ready to dive into my quest of seeking out this God who captivated my soul. I was in awe of the prophetic. However, I was more in awe of the God who revealed such secrets to a mere man. I knew with assurance that I was on the heart of God.

And this is where the journey began. The altar experience wasn't a church encounter of me giving my life to God then snatching it back. On that day, I memorialized myself and trusted God with the life He apprehended. That day I said RIP Sophia as I laid down my life, and prepared to walk into my assignment in which God sent me into the earth to complete. God never showed me the whole picture, however as I look back over my life, I am in awe of how heaven delivered a mighty transformation through me.

In this book, I want to walk you through my journey towards reclaiming my feminine identity. I want to reveal how God snatched my identity back from the enemy by destroying his system. I want to share my process of how God walked me out of the culture of homosexuality and masculinity. Deliverance from homosexuality and perversion was one thing. However, it was God's desire to deliver me from the culture by removing all residue and traces from me internally and externally that connected me to my past. There is a process after the altar, and it's not easy, but it's worth it.

The Day After

So what really happens after leaving the altar? What next? I mean the day after I was still unconscious and numb from my altar experience. I did more than say the sinner's prayer. I gave my life completely to God. I was confused on what to do next because nothing had externally changed about me. I mean I had no idea what to expect. What was I supposed to do now with all of this God, yet I still looked and felt the same. My heart yearned for God, but my body was craving something else. I looked around and remembered saying to myself, " I need help. How am I supposed to walk through this process without a manual? Where is the blueprint? Who can I call? Who can help me?" I wondered where the delivered people were. Where is my help? I wondered how in the world I was going to figure this out, then I just brushed it off and said, " I guess He would finish it. He began the work, so it's on Him to finish it."

When I woke up the next morning, the first thing I did was check the mirror. I was still the same person. I was expecting to see a change, especially since I felt a change in my heart. I can remember doing a pat down trying to assess if anything had changed externally. To my surprise, I looked the same, spoke the same, walked the same, and of course had the same sexual desires for the same sex. I couldn't help but believe the words of the enemy that quoted over and over, "The God I bowed to on Sunday was the God who abandoned me on Monday." I believed the voice of the enemy because his words were so loud, and so realistic. I didn't have any substance to stand on, and couldn't defeat the vicious voice of Satan as he pressured me with words of defeat. He talked so bad about God, and made sure he painted the picture of God not being a fulfilling God, but an abandoning God. I felt ashamed, embarrassed, and all alone as I was left to fight an enemy that was bigger than me. His words felt like a sucker punch to the face, and all the butterflies I felt Sunday slowly drifted away. I immediately found myself questioning my salvation. I also wondered what good could possibly come out of my life. As I pondered this, I heard in a still small voice, "Everything good could happen." The voice of the Lord rescued me from defeat, as His words entered my heart until the very sound of hell was demolished. I must admit I was intrigued with how powerful the voice of God was, that when He spoke everything remained silent. I didn't have to argue with hell any longer. When God spoke, darkness fled. It appeared weird that each time my back was against the wall, the voice of God would come in and literally scatter my enemies.

I could recall craving to hear the voice of God. I would do whatever it took to hear His voice, so I began to develop a habit of seeking Him, even if it meant rising and seeking Him early. I would wake up with this urge to locate God as if He was my GPS for my day. I sought Him for direction. My entire life depended on Him, and I was determined to find Him. I knew I couldn't possibly do anything without Him, so I ensured that God would be my friend in the earth to go before me. I would rise early and go to bed late, caught up in this discovery of the supernatural realm. This habit went on for months until I recognized the voice of God consistently. After months of seeking the voice of the Lord, each day His voice would get louder and louder. I was learning to distinguish the voice of God from the voice of the enemy. I didn't know much about the Bible, so I would dive into the Word so that I would have a weapon to use against the enemy. To be honest y'all I was a fighter in the natural, so warfare was something I dived right into. I knew that I couldn't combat the enemy in my flesh. Therefore the Word of God became my armor. I put on the full armor of God according to Ephesians 6:10-18. I wasn't studying to learn scripture to impress my neighbor; I was learning Word to defeat the enemy that was bullying me. I learned fast that this battle is not mine, but it belonged to the Lord, so fighting became my new norm. I was determined to wipe him out.

The scripture that saved my life was John1:1, which declares, "I am the word." Immediately a hunger stirred and reading became a part of my private time. I had no idea that I was having devotion with God, and He was pleased with the time we were spending. It's like God was grooming me for Himself. It was imperative for me to discern His voice so that I would be secure in my process, as I walked out my deliverance. Any wrong moves or delayed obedience had the power to abort my process, so developing a personal relationship was critical. I do believe that it's key to be connected to leadership, attend church, and fellowship, however, it's God's desire that we prioritize and develop a personal relationship with the Holy Spirit. God is the Word. If you want to know God, find Him in His Word. My destiny depended on me hearing, knowing, and perceiving His voice. Man has the ability to disappoint and let you down, so I put my entire trust in God. Let's dive deeper.

THE IMPORTANCE OF KNOWING HIS VOICE

When walking through deliverance, there are many voices that are speaking and dictating your next move. The Bible declares, "A sheep hears My voice, and will follow." God is very strategic in the relationship process. Activating your ear to hearing, discerning, and following His voice are connected and vital in the deliverance process. God is aware that you will follow what you hear, and what you hear, you will obey. The Holy Spirit becomes your counselor, and teacher during this process, and He is intentional with familiarizing you with His voice. He takes on the role of Truth, and will lead and guide you into all truth to possess your freedom; a freedom that's unrestricted and unrestrained.

Obedience is also connected to hearing. God is aware of who you are, and how you respond. Remember He knew you before the foundation of the world and knows how you respond. I can remember feeling I was in a supernatural boot camp early in my walk. While I was developing a personal relationship with God, I was beginning to have encounters with Him that kept drawing me back for more. I began to have open visions, visitations, and dreams. The spiritual realm was opening up, and I was overwhelmed with reverence. I refused to tell others about my encounters to keep from being judged or being called "weird." I didn't understand the prophetic, and I hadn't been trained in it, so I wasn't sure what to do with all these experiences. My development came directly from the Holy Spirit Himself. I became His student, and He became my Teacher. I was desperate for more. I was beginning to crave His presence, which kept pushing me to pursuit. I pursued God, and suddenly the tables were turning, God began to pursue me. It was like a crush, leading to a relationship. We were totally into one another on such a personal level, that God became my personal friend—the one in whom I put all my trust and confidence in.

The more I sought God, the more the encounters intensified. I never said a word to anyone. I feared informing anyone of my encounters with God because I didn't think anyone would believe me, especially because I didn't physically look saved. Heck, to be honest, it was hard for me to believe God would visit a wretch like me. That's the beauty of the mystery of God. He loves you through the good, bad, and the ugly. God takes your surrendering personal, and it takes a level of submission to truly walk out the culture of sin, to embrace the culture of the kingdom. Deliverance is often aborted or miscarried at the hands of interference, which causes an interruption in your process. So God establishes a personal relationship with you. The veil is broken. You don't have to go through man to reach God. You have access to boldly approach the throne. The blood was the sacrifice that granted me access. God immediately makes a distinction by separating His voices from any other voice that would attempt to arise during your process of deliverance.

The voice of the Lord is the prerequisite for surviving after the altar. I had to learn the voice of God in order for progression to take place in my life. Deliverance wasn't a one-time event where I went to the altar and poof all of my demons were gone. There was a progressive process that happened after God required me to know, discover, and perceive His voice. I learned to treat the awareness of His voice as a necessity. I didn't religiously arise to seek Him for any reason other than to find Him. It was something internal provoking me into His presence.

One thing about me is that I have an addictive personality. The enemy always used addictions against me to bind me to darkness. Once I tasted of God's goodness, an addiction began manifesting, and I longed for His voice and His words. God took me under His wing and walked me through deliverance beautifully. Many couldn't understand nor comprehend my process because it was personal. God did it, that no man can boast! I began to walk in sonship. I was adopted into the kingdom of God and became a joint heir with Christ. The adoption in which I am able to cry Abba Father legalized me, and gave me access to be BENEFICIARY of everything my Father left for me. I learned to submit to the process.

Right now, if you are reading this book, I recommend you stop reading and Selah. Praise God for taking on the role of the Father and agreeing to finish what He began in your life. He who began a good work will complete it. (Philippians 1:6). Give God the glory for revealing His voice to you and taking on the responsibility to give you hope and a future. Praise God for your process. If you made it to the altar, that's the biggest step of your life. Don't you dare despise small beginnings in your process. You're trying to figure out the big picture when God is trying to give you joy in your journey. Shut your ears to the false voices attempting to be God in your life, and open your ears to the true and living God. You may not feel saved, but your confession makes you right with God. The blood is your covering and gives you access to establish a foundation with the Holy Spirit now by pressing into His presence. Stop trying to visualize who you will become, and allow God to walk you into who you shall become. I declare that your ears are open and active to hear and obey the voice of the Lord. You can do this! Don't give up, don't throw in the towel, keep pressing. God has plans for your life!

Come with me as I share more of my personal story. I want to share my journey with you on how God walked me through homosexuality and masculinity by hearing, following and obeying His voice throughout the entire process. Take God out of the box, and witness the transformational power of deliverance.

Two

DISMANTLING THE CULTURE OF HOMOSEXUALITY

I CAN RECALL NUMEROUS OCCASIONS WHEN KIDS WOULD walk up to me or ask their parents if I was a girl or a boy. Going into the women's restroom was complete torture, as kids stared me down, and women looked me up and down trying to identify my gender. Parents would grab their daughters, while kids pointed and expressed, "Mommy why is a boy in the girl's restroom?" Immediately I would attempt to talk because although I was extremely masculine, my voice remained squeaky and girly. Once I opened my mouth the kids would look confused and stare at me with the weirdest look of disapproval. I didn't pay it much mind. I was living my life and really didn't care who questioned my gender. However, after giving my life to God, these moments became uncomfortable. There were times when I liked confusing people about my gender, and there were times when it was quite embarrassing.

I found that people would often ask about my gender because they didn't know how to identify me. If you are not familiar with the homosexual community, it's difficult to comprehend their language, and the numerous titles to identify their role and function in the lifestyle. I believe many people would ask if I was a girl or a boy to avoid offending me, or because they just didn't know. It was hard to tell my gender if you didn't know me, didn't hear me speak, or if you saw me from a distance. I had a bald fade, I wore my clothes three sizes too big, and baggy pants to ensure you could see my Ralph Lauren boxers. My breasts were patted down with a tight sports bra, and I held my crotch as if I really had something to hold. I walked hard. My mannerisms were hard, and I enjoyed the tiny little hairs growing under my chin. It made me feel like I had a beard growing in. The level of deception was real. In the homosexual community, I was known as a stud, a masculine lesbian viewed as a male. I took on the role as the man in my relationships. I was dominant, the provider, and very aggressive. Don't get me wrong; there are feminine lesbians. However, in this particular story, I want to focus on the masculine stud.

Early on I learned the role of the stud from my experience playing basketball, and being around veteran studs who were able to train me up in the way I was advised to go. I was very comfortable in men's clothing, and I forced myself to look harder than I actually was. I went the extra mile trying to be a man. There was nothing feminine about me. I even convinced myself at one point that I was one of the guys. Spending years in the homosexual lifestyle, I learned to embrace my masculinity and developed the mannerism of manhood. Being a stud had become my identity, I didn't know myself outside of who I had worked so hard to become. I was in the prime of my sexuality and was developing new levels of darkness that would usher me deeper into darkness. Homosexuals take pride in the slogan, "Gay Pride," because that's exactly what it is; happy and proud to be gay. It's like earning stripes for being dark, the darker you're into it, the greater you are respected by your peers. Conversion power was like a badge of honor, and along the journey, I had become gay and proud. I was an advocate of my sexuality and was unashamed. I was always ready to contend with anyone who brought a judgment against the identity I'd grown to embrace.

My behavior as a stud was deeper than how I dressed. There was something internal that triggered external manifestations. I had a dose of demonic adrenaline that gave me momentum on how to act and conduct myself. I groomed and prepared myself before going out in public. I wouldn't be caught in public without a sports bra, my baggy shorts, or jeans. I needed to be in stud role at all times. The biggest struggle was trying to adjust my vocal cords to sound masculine, but the harder I tried, the squeaker my voice would become. I would often get frustrated at the uniqueness of my voice tone. I had some weird scratchy pitch, so I had to make up for it in my style and behavior. I was aggressive, and my body language had a specific posture when sitting, standing or relaxing. I had a posture when I was kicking it with my guys, or when I was conversing with women. The only reason I smoked weed was because it added to my swag, and intoxicated me from the reality that I was trying hard to be someone I wasn't. I was in performance role at all times. I had to put on the act of being a man.

When people would question my gender, it confirmed I was on track and appeared manly enough to confuse others. I developed the culture of my sexuality. Just like an American is proud to be an American, as a homosexual I was proud to be a homosexual. Here's a reason why one must have wisdom when ministering to a homosexual. Homosexuality is rooted in pride and deception, and a wrong move could hinder the ministry encounter. You couldn't just walk up to me and say God wants to deliver you from your struggle. I didn't see my lifestyle as a struggle, because this was my culture. My identity was bound to the lifestyle I'd grown accustomed to living. I didn't see myself as being in any struggles. Many would say I was going to hell, and would focus on the consequences I would receive if I didn't change my life. That charge was not persuasive because hell wasn't a reality for me. When I went to the altar, it wasn't because I was tired of being gay. I didn't even know what deliverance was, so that wasn't the case. I was apprehended by a power that was bigger than Sophia. I didn't count the cost of what would be next concerning my life. I was just obeying the voice that beckoned me to come.

When God invited me to the altar, He knew exactly what He was doing even when I didn't. I knew I would have to eventually give up my same-sex desire, but I wasn't giving up the Stud Life. Crazy huh? I was willing to give up same-sex attraction if He took away the desire, but I was holding on to my appearance and identity. I can even recall saying to God, "You can deliver me, but don't you dare touch my identity." My personality was wrapped in my identity, and I didn't know who I was outside of being a stud. I wanted to give God my internal being, but externally I wanted that part of me to remain unbothered. I held on to my identity with clenched fists, refusing to let go. God is so awesome. He knows exactly what He's doing. I often laugh because you won't always see the big picture, but God knows the end before the beginning.

God dealt with the cultural state of my mind. God didn't focus on stripping me without rescuing me from the culture in which I resided. When God escorts you *from* a place, it's to bring you *into* a place. I lived a homosexual lifestyle most of my high school, and college years. I grew accustomed to residing in the stronghold of homosexuality and perversion. I wasn't just gay. I invested years being an agent for the powers of darkness. I was a principality, sucking the life out of many and turning them out to darkness. Everything about me was a reflection of my residence. If a person saw me, they knew the lifestyle I lived without me saying a word. The culture of my identity revealed where I was from. The residue of sin was my identification of the cultural background I resided in.

It's like being born in the United States, and at age 13 your parents move you to China. You live in China from age

13-23. That's living a decade in a foreign country during the most impressionable years of your life. In this transition you adapt to the mores of the Chinese and take on the social mindset of that environment. You're no longer trying to live like an American citizen while in China. You learn to adapt and begin to transform your life that's conducive to your living environment. You learn the rules of China. You pick up the language, mannerisms, and style of that country. If you return to America after a decade of living in China, it will take awhile to adjust to the new atmosphere, region, and culture. You would have to learn and adjust to the American way. That's how it is for a homosexual who goes to the altar, gives their life to God, and prepares for the journey of deliverance. The very culture has to be destroyed. I experienced homesickness. There were times during the process that I wanted to go back. I definitely had to be trained on the new life I was living.

When God called me to the altar, I didn't have time to prepare for relocating in the spirit. I didn't have time to fully count up the cost. I moved abruptly. Only God has the power and authority to uproot you from one place to the other. Since God called me, I depended on Him to establish and fully furnish me. I began to trust God with the process of my journey. Was it easy? Absolutely not! But it was beautiful witnessing the ongoing progression of God molding and shaping me into the woman of God He called me to be.

BUTTERFLY EFFECT

Romans 12:2, "Do not conform to the pattern of this world, but be transformed by the renewing of your mind." Have you ever seen a butterfly? The metamorphosis of a butterfly is beautiful. Before the butterfly grows into an adult, they must go through four stages. A lot of times we embrace the butterfly but abandon the other three stages. Before that butterfly develops levels of beauty, there are seasons of ugliness. At each stage, as a butterfly is prepared to manifest, each goal is different. That's exactly how it was for me as God took me through a series of stages that had goals at every level. I heard many people prophesy to me that I would be a butterfly, but to be honest, I didn't have any idea how God could take someone so masculine and beautify them.

We often celebrate the butterfly because that's the stage where the butterfly is ready to fly. I witnessed hell as I went through my egg, larva (caterpillar), and Chrysalis stages. People were pressuring me to manifest my deliverance by proving I was saved through my external appearance. They were making statements like, "I wonder what Sophia would look like in a skirt. When are you going to get a man? When are you going to wear make-up and do your hair?" What they didn't know is I was in my stages of internal development, and God was the potter. They were connecting my deliverance to outer manifestation when God clearly states He weighs the matters of the heart over outer appearance. So many times church leadership, peers, and family need to see the manifestation before they believe you're free. God

works in miracles, signs, and wonders. He takes the foolish
things to confound the wise. So while many were waiting
to see me a certain way to believe, God was dismantling the
internal culture of a lifestyle that was unseen. The process of
deliverance is immediate for some, however, for me, it was a
journey of submission. I learned to submit to God, resist the
devil, and watch him flee.

The most vulnerable stage of my life was during the
chrysalis phase. I was a caterpillar, done growing. However,
a chrysalis was the Holy Spirit that covered me as changes
were occurring internally. The Holy Spirit covered and pro-
tected me from the warfare around me, and no one was able
to comprehend where I was in the spirit realm. During this
phase people were cutting me off, persecuting me, and using
words and accusations to kill me. At this phase I was totally delivered from same-sex attraction and was living pure
before God. However, my appearance didn't reflect my confession, so those close to me still labeled me as gay. I would
get so discouraged during this stage because I was free from
sin, I just wasn't delivered from the culture. The Holy Spirit had to come in and rescue me Himself to keep me from
going back, due to the accusations from the saints. I was
kept from being hurt, and guarded against offense. I kept
growing, while many were trying to kill me. I took rest in
the Spirit, as change was taking place. While I was wrapped
in the chrysalis stage, the butterfly in me was growing and
developing. However my revealing took time, God's time.

Let me encourage you. Don't kill the butterfly while they are in the caterpillar state. And if you are the caterpillar, don't come out of hiding until God gives you your wings to soar. Your internal and external beauty is in His plan, and in His timing. Don't give up on your process because others don't understand where you are in the spirit realm. Keep giving God access to your life, and watch Him manifest you internally and externally. Persecution will come from those who are closest to you, however, keep pushing, keep soaring, keep yielding, and keep growing. You are being equipped to be the syllabus for the next generation.

Even as a butterfly has stages, so does a homosexual who is walking through their stages of deliverance. Follow me deeper into more of my story.

Dismantling of the Homosexual Culture

I am so thankful that I learned to develop an ear to hear God, so I was able to pace myself to yield to each process of my deliverance. I was able to heed His voice and follow. The stages of my life were real gruesome, and I wondered if it was possible to ever live up to His expectations. God reminded me that it's not by might, nor by power, but by His Spirit, I could do it. My flesh was weak, and my spirit was willing, so I buckled down and watched God work on my life. I took the passenger seat, put on a seat belt, and literally watched God move upon my life this entire process, and guess what, He's still not through with me. I am still progressing in areas of my life.

God is so smooth. He has a way of walking you through deliverance in a way that's brilliant. God didn't deal with me like a judge, banging a gavel and dictating in a harsh tone do this or do that. God was such a gentlemen every step of the way. Remember I mentioned earlier how God dealt with me developing an ear to hear because hearing leads to obedience. That was the strategy God used to walk me through deliverance. I heard, I obeyed, and God delivered.

The dismantling process began as God strategically began to change my culture, and I yielded. God invaded my space, and when the Holy Spirit moved in, the Spirit began to remove all particles of my former state. When I accepted Christ as my personal savior it was more than words; it was an invitation of moving God in and allowing Him to move things out. It involved welcoming the Holy Spirit to live, dwell and abide in me. I was granting the Spirit access to move in, and when the Spirit moves in, everything else that's not like God is cast out. God became the landlord over my soul, and He served eviction notices to all unauthorized demonic tenants. The cast-out was real. There were times when God gave eviction notices, and there were times He kicked the enemy out instantaneously. God is committed to purifying His temple because you are the temple of the Holy Spirit.

Music Was the First to Go

Music was big for me back in the day. I was a bootleg CD fanatic. People would burn multiple songs on a CD for me, which gave me access to all my favorite artists for cheap.

I loved me some Lil Wayne, TI, Twista, Juvenile, R. Kelley, Silk, Dru Hill, and Ray J. Lil Wayne was the only CD I would purchase because I loved him so much, and wanted to support him. I would literally leave church, get inside my car, and immediately put on a Lil Wayne track. The very revelation I received was snatched before I got home, and instead of singing *Jesus Loves Me This I Know*, I was vibing to, "Go DJ, that's my DJ." I had a thing for collecting CD's. Music dictated my mood and set my atmosphere. The enemy doesn't care how he enters your life, he just needs an open door, and with or without permission, he enters and attempts to launch his plan against you. Music is a door opener for the enemy to enter at will. Music isn't just singing a song. It's a luring spirit that escorts you into a place of violence, perversion, depression, sadness, and so much more. Music has a driving ability, and is able to transport you to a destination called sin. Just think about your favorite song, and ask yourself why it's your favorite song. Usually, it's because it creates a mood. It alters your mood, or sets a specific atmosphere that's conducive to what you're feeling. Music is powerful, and the enemy uses this power to keep demonic doors open that would give him access to enter your life.

The enemy put in overtime trying to find loopholes to recapture my soul. I had Lil-Wayne CD's in my car, and I had the same music downloaded on my Xbox in the house. I would come inside the house, turn on my Xbox, grab the remote, and begin blasting the music as loud as I could. The music would capture my soul and attention instantly. I would go from rapping, to slow jamming, and next thing you know, I'd created moods that either made me want to smoke, go to the club, or find a woman to sleep with. Music was like a crutch that helped me limp into places I didn't need to go. Music was like therapy that escalated and de-escalated my emotions. I didn't utilize God. Music had become my God that I was using to deal with my issues. Some of you may ask, is music that bad for you? I can only express that it was negative for me, and God was dismantling anything that was put before Him. Music was a driving force that kept an open door for the enemy to come in.

After about six months of this ongoing battle, something supernatural happened. I was in the car with my two God-daughters, blasting my music as I drove to the car wash. The sun was shining, and everybody was outside hanging on the block. I was cruising in my Chevy Impala, tinted windows, feeling fresh, as I headed to clean and detail my whip before hitting a few blocks. As we pulled into the car wash, I heard this still small voice say, "Sophia throw away all of your CD's." I paused, looked around, and thought to myself, "What is that?" The voice was gentle, yet the authority was strong as I heard, "Sophia throw away your music." I responded out loud by stating, "What music?" The voice declared, "All of your music, get rid of it all." I put my hand over my face, looked up, and said, "Not again God." I was beginning to get used to these random moments when God would show up and direct me to do something. I paused, kept my foot on the brakes, and tried to think away the voice.

My Goddaughters looked at one another, trying to figure out who I was talking to. I laughed and thought I was
tweaking, so I shrugged my shoulders, and thought to myself that I was going too deep. The voice came clear again,
and this time I said, "I won't throw them away. I'll give them
away." I had way too much music to throw away. I then
advised my Goddaughters that the Lord was speaking to me
and telling me to get rid of my music. They were surprised,
looked at one another, and said, "Wow Sophia. Are you really throwing this music away?" I immediately responded
with an act of obedience. I grabbed all of my music, from
multiple compartments in my car, gathered them together in
both hands, walked to the large green trash, and threw them
all away. I smiled, shook my head, and assured the girls that
God had a plan behind it all. I resumed with washing my
car, listening to the sound of birds and crickets.

As I was leaving the car wash, I ran into one of the el-
der's of the church. We spoke briefly, side by side from one
another's vehicle. She pulled up with a huge smile, saying,
"How you doing Sophia?" I sarcastically looked at her, and
expressed that I had just thrown away all of my CD's and I
didn't have any music to listen to. She smiled and asked if I
wanted to borrow her Martha Munizzi CD. I said, "Oh yes,
please." An overwhelming excitement hit me, as I forgot
about what I threw away, and anxiously grabbed the CD. I
immediately put the CD on in the car, and put on the song
that I had gotten saved to, *God Is Here*. My entire mannerism

and countenance shifted. I noticed an immediate change. I refused to hit extra blocks. I adjusted my seat from leaning backward to sitting up and drove straight home. When I arrived at the house, I cleared my Xbox as well, and completely obeyed God.

I was so amazed that God had spoken to me and that I had obeyed. I didn't question God, I didn't procrastinate or argue, I simply obeyed. This minor adjustment caused me to set the atmosphere in my car, and inside my home with worship and praise. I was reminded of God inviting me to the altar, so I played the song God Is Here over and over again. I also fell in love with the songs It's a New Season, and Your Latter Will Be Greater. I began to sing these songs and declare these words out of my mouth during times of prayer and devotion to God. I played the gospel track on my Xbox, and my home was filled with praise. God was taking over in such a unique way, and I loved how deliverance from rap and R&B was shifting my life. Now don't get me wrong, and assume that I am advising you to get rid of your music. Remember this is my story, and I am shedding light on the process God took me through.

After getting tired of listening to the same track, I went to the Christian bookstore and purchased a Shirley Caesar cd. I sure wish the song "You name it" had been out back in the day. I would have been jamming. Over time my CD collection became compiled of all Gospel, and I never looked back. It's miraculous. There was no pressure from outsiders on changing my music, no conviction, and no preparation. It was just God speaking, and me hearing and obeying. Do you see how it works, and why it's important to develop an ear to hear the voice of God? God trained my ear in the beginning because as I mentioned earlier hearing is connected to obeying. I often wonder what would have happened along the journey if I had disobeyed his voice. I wonder if my process would have been delayed? Would I have developed so wonderfully? Only God knows. However, I want you to Selah this moment and focus on God's voice and what He's asking you to do. Many people struggle and try to find ways to keep their desires, and serve God without making any sacrifices. When you do this, a power struggle occurs where your flesh wars with the Spirit, and who you serve you will obey. If you live by the flesh, you will die by flesh. If you walk by the Spirit, you will live by the Spirit. I chose to walk and live by the Spirit.

Music was a hobby for me, and I often spent idol time listening to it. When the music barrier was dismantled, my idle time was spent seeking, serving, and devoting myself to God. I would turn on my music, grab a journal, lay out a sheet as my threshing floor, and cry out to God for help. I would spend hours in prayer and devotion. I would go to bed at midnight and arise at 4 a.m. seeking God. I was so desperate to trace the God who captured my heart. During my times of prayer, I would drift off and take flight in my imagination, picturing God face to face. While in His presence I shared my secrets, my hurts, my desires, and the pain of suffering significant loss. God was so gracious and beautiful that each time He would rescue me with His words. I was beginning to read the Bible, and the scriptures were coming alive. I spent endless nights reading the Gospels, and meditating on Jesus, salvation, and the love of the Father towards me. My independent time with the Lord was building supernatural muscle in the spirit. Although there was no change in my external behaviors, my spirit was getting stronger and stronger. God became first, and suddenly my social habits began to shift. The only time I was having access to worldly music was when I found myself in the club.

Social Habits Dismantled

For months after the altar, I found myself falling, slipping, going to clubs, drinking, and hanging out in the streets. I was still known in the community as a stud, and highly respected by both males and females. I was still attracted to the same sex for about three years post altar, even though for months and even a year I was able to avoid slipping into sexual sin, and walked in purity. I was trying hard to be obedient to God, and there were times my flesh was able to go without sex. I knew that God disapproved of fornication and same-sex attraction, so my denial of the flesh had more to do with obeying God than me actually being delivered. Each time I fell, I found myself beating myself up, and saying over and over, I'm not saved. There is no way I could be saved and still have same-sex attractions. I would go before God crying and asking why He wasn't removing the desire. Why was I still having these desires when He gave me His

Spirit? It didn't make sense. I didn't know how to work out my own salvation. I didn't know how to be strong by getting back up. One fall would set me back for weeks. I would find myself depressed and struggling with this deliverance stuff and God. How could you be delivered and still want the things you were delivered from? Each time I went to God, He would wipe me off with His blood, pick my chin up, look me in the eye, and say, "For I know the plans I have for You." I couldn't comprehend God. I was feeling traumatized because I couldn't put a finger on the mind of God. I learned early in my walk to keep going to God, and keep making your request known to Him. I bothered God so much with a desire to be free, until God declared loudly, "Daughter you are free." How was I free when I felt so bound?

With each fall I continued to get stronger. I was learning to discern when I was about to fall before I fell. I would try to kick this addiction like a drug addict trying to kick a habit. When I fell, the binge was real, as I said to myself, "Well I've sinned so I might as well go all out." The enemy tormented me and tried to block me from God with words like, "Girl what are you doing? You know you still gay. God hates you because if He loved you, He would save you." I began to take it personally when the enemy would speak so ill of my God. I would argue back and declare that he was a lie, and remind hell that I have access to something he will never be granted and that's repentance. When I used scripture against the enemy, power and authority came upon me.

God began to strip me of social habits that were keeping me in a state of falling. There was a time I was at the club with one of my guy friends, and we went to two gay clubs in one night. The first club was in St. Louis, Missouri where we did the norm. Danced, sipped a drink of Malibu and pineapple juice, chilled and had a great time. While in the club a group of drag queens came out, and began dancing on the dance floor, and suddenly the music amplified, the bright lights moved fast, and all I could think was, "I can't wait to leave." I was beginning to feel uncomfortable and didn't know what was happening. I looked around and said, "These people tripping. Why are we all being so fake." Everyone was dressed up in attire opposite of their gender, even me, and all I could do was shake my head. I thought it was the liquor getting to me, but I was zooming in on deception; women wanting to be men, and men wanting to be women. It felt delusional, but I couldn't trip, I had to go along with the flow. After leaving this particular club, we hit up a gay club that was open from 3 a.m. until 6 a.m. We were both tipsy, but the clubbing continued. This club had the same atmosphere, perversion right before my eyes. I remember sitting at the bar and falling asleep. We departed, and when I arrived home, I felt so tired and dirty. I recalled the scene of what I witnessed at the club and kept thinking of the deception. I was beginning to get uncomfortable in my own skin, but I couldn't let it be known.

Over a period of time my social habits began to shift. I found myself spending time with God. I would get so caught up reading and praying that three days would go by and I would be in the house without a care about hanging out. Eventually my desires for going out changed, drinking and smoking stopped, and demonic social habits were dismantled. I would get calls from friends about going out, and wouldn't feel pressured to go. I didn't have to cut my friends off, my friends started cutting me off. When our common interests shifted, they separated from me. I realized that the more time I spent with God, the brighter my light was becoming. It was difficult for me to recognize my light but others did. Darkness can't dwell in light. My circle changed, and I was developing friendships with others who were in church. After a while, my old friends would ask about my salvation, and would say, "You'll be back." One thing they didn't know about me was that when I'm into something, I'm fully committed. I give my heart to anything I'm committed to, and God had my whole heart. I was devoted to progression and believed that He knew the plans He had for me. How they would work out, I had no clue, but my faith declared me righteous.

God replaced my social life on the streets, by giving me assignments in the church to remain focused. I was helping in the media department, which resulted in me attending praise team practice, and faithfully being at church. I enjoyed my job and took turning the mic up and down very seriously. There were times I would intentionally turn the mic down when some of the ladies were singing, and if my apostle said anything I didn't want to hear, I turned his mic down too. I became intrigued with corporate prayer and Bible study. I began attending Morning Prayer at 5 a.m., and would awake at 4 a.m., head out the house by 4:30 a.m. and would ride around the community praying. I wanted to speak in tongues so badly that I was trying to get a head start to see if my tongues would fall upon like the day of Pentecost before arriving at the church. I admired the prayer leaders and loved to hear them pray. They prayed so strong, loud, and with authority, I would say to myself, "I want to pray like that." I would be into it, and when it ended I didn't stop praying, I went home and continued to pray. I began to ask God for tongues, but it took awhile before the tongues manifested. The enemy tormented me about not speaking in tongues. I felt I wasn't saved because I wasn't manifesting tongues which is the initial evidence of being baptized in the Holy Spirit. Then one day the Lord began to teach me about the 7-fold Holy Spirit, and how He wanted me to have a full outpouring of His Spirit. I learned that tongues are the evidence, but I had the spirit of wisdom, knowledge, under-standing, might, counsel, fear, and the Spirit of the Lord. I then ordered the book *Good Morning Holy Spirit* by Benny Hinn, and my seeking for the friendship of the Spirit up-graded. I found myself entering into God's presence, and it felt so heavenly. I would get caught up in devotion, and not want to come out of His presence to deal with my flesh.

God began to teach me how to walk in the Spirit, and as I learned to walk in the Spirit, I was no longer yielding to my flesh. As my relationship with the Spirit intensified,

His request became louder and bolder. Here's a moment, I didn't foresee. One random day, God spoke to me and said, "Sophia, throw away all sexual toys." I stopped in my tracks because now God was stripping me of an item that made me feel the most masculine. I didn't want to get rid of my sexual object. I needed it for a just in case moment. But the voice was so clear and direct. Without much hesitation, I obeyed God. I threw my sexual object in the trash and never looked back. Once God stripped me of the object that made me feel aggressive, masculine, and dominate, I was left empty handed. I couldn't understand what God was doing, but I obeyed. There were two occasions, I felt like going to a sex store and getting another one, but the conviction was stronger than ever, and I never looked back. I never entertained the thought of obtaining sexual objects again, and that door of perversion was closed.

Stripping a stud of her sexual items is like taking away an instrument from a musician; it goes against the essential expression of who they are. God dismantled the stronghold that connected me to masculinity, when I let those sex toys go.

What About Friends and Relationships?

Many wonder if I had to walk away from friendships and relationships, once I became saved. To be perfectly honest, I didn't run around looking to break off or put an end to my friendships or relationships. Nor did I have a sit-down talk concerning break-ups, and I didn't tell all my homies, "Yo I'm saved now, so we can't hang." Everything in my process was supernatural. Relationships that didn't have a foundation established blew away with no sign of resistance. It was easy to walk away from relationships that were only based on us having one thing in common, perversion. However, friendships that were rooted and grounded in love beyond sex, sexual attraction, and perversion, were friendships I was able to maintain. People often questioned my friendships based on my sexuality, however just because I was gay didn't mean I was sleeping with every person I had a friendship with. Many would ask how I could remain friends with someone I had once been intimate with, and my response would be, "Can a drug addict be delivered from crack, and not smoke again? Can an alcoholic be delivered and not drink again? Can a liar be delivered from lying and not lie again?" The answer is absolutely, but it is necessary that you obey God throughout the entire process, and allow Him to unyoke you from ungodly soul ties, to ensure that the very forces of evil are uprooted and overthrown.

Because homosexuality has a stigma attached, "Once gay, always gay," many are deceived to believe that a homosexual can't be free. At the beginning of my deliverance, due to the pressure of others making me feel that it was impossible to be friends with other homosexuals, I was driven to a place of trying to cut off relationships on my own. I immediately went into survival mode and planned strategies in my head that would disconnect me from relationships that I had established over the years. Being that I was a people person and had many friends, I struggled with trying to figure out how I would be able to manage friendships without being accused of sleeping with them. There is a stigma that people believe if you are gay, you automatically want anything that's of the same sex. Can I set the record straight for a second? Just because a person is gay, doesn't mean they are attracted to you. Homosexuals have preferences and options, just as heterosexuals. So I was able to quickly adjust to being a friend, and not a lover with the women God blessed to be a part of my life. Instead of trying to do it on my own, I sought God for guidance, strength, and courage to close doors that I was keeping open.

God blew on my relationships in drastic steps by allowing me to renounce covenants, contracts, and words I spoke during my times of intimacy. I renounced and denounced every word and prayed for ungodly soul ties to be destroyed. I had no idea that my prayers were literally moving heaven, and God was responding. One day I was driving on the interstate, and my brother-in-law was trailing me. He began blowing and waving for me to pull over. I thought to myself, why can't this wait, I mean we are on the highway, and he can't just wait. I pull over, and he hands me a book called *Prayers that Deroute Demons* by Apostle John Eckhardt. I asked him why he was giving me this book because it looked like a book of scriptures, and I didn't want to read it. He said the Lord told him to give it to me. I grabbed the book and said, "Wow this book must be special if he chased me on the interstate to give it to me." To my surprise when I arrived home, I began to dig into that book. I started out praying a few of the prayers and taking notes. Then one day I started reading about specific sexual demons *Incubus* and *Succubus*. I had no clue what these spirits were, so I looked them up and did research so I could pray with knowledge. When I tell you the power of God was manifesting, I literally prayed the entire book over and over until I began memorizing those prayers. I fasted for a whole year doing fruits and vegetables, and refusing to watch television until I knew every ungodly connection to the past was destroyed. Separation wasn't easy, but when I allowed God to do it, He made a beautiful transition.

God had me get rid of television, and instead of watching TV, I spent hours in prayer seeking His face. See people this wasn't a joke for me. I wanted to be free, and I simply learned the power of obedience. I invested time in God's face, and held Him accountable for getting me out of the strongholds that held me like concrete. Many of you may look at this and say, I ain't doing all that, but if you want to be free you would go to the source who holds the key to your freedom. God is strategic and has a way of getting you hooked and addicted to Him until you will forsake everything to follow. Yes, you will struggle, you will fall, you will have setbacks, but you will always return home. Tasting of God's goodness is the greatest taste one can ever experience, and once you have one hit you won't be the same. It's an addicting taste that has you on a wild goose chase. Sin can't even keep you from coming back into His presence requesting of more of Him. So like an addict I kept coming back for hits, and after each hit, I would experience breakthroughs. Always remember that when God request for you to give up a thing, He's going to replace it with something far better than what you're attempting to keep. After breaking into strong encounters with God and several strippings, everything connected to me broke off.

When people attempt to carry out dismantles, they tend to do it prematurely because of the pressure of outside voices, and eventually those who were once out of the closet, find themselves saved and in the closet. I refused to get free than find myself bound in secret. If God was in it, I trusted Him to deliver me, not make me fight the battles in my flesh. This battle was the Lord's and not Sophia's. I didn't choose God, but God chose me. I put the pressure on God to do the delivering, so I wouldn't be forced to suppress demons, and not be delivered. It's easy to go on a fast and stop a habit, however, when you stop a habit in your flesh, the weight of sin comes back seven times worse.

LANGUAGE

My mouth was foul. I was great at word organization to curse you out. I would often use profanity to express my feelings. Profanity was like a secondary language. After a few years of walking through my deliverance, God began to deal with my mouth. God placed coal upon my lips, and purified my mouth. The Lord began to declare that I would prophesy and be a voice in the earth, but my lips had to be clean. I allowed the Lord to purify my lips and began to pray that He would put a guard around my mouth. My language that was so foreign and so far from God began to change from cursing to blessing. I learned to use my mouth to make bold declarations over my life. I can recall spending time prophesying and pretending to preach in front of thousands. I learned the power of the tongue and used my words wisely. Over time as my language in the Spirit increased, my vocabulary was filled with praise.

When God changes your language, your conversation with others changes as well. I began to speak about God, and before I knew it, that was my conversation. Others were starting to recognize the growth and maturity based on my ability to dialogue so freely without using profanity. People would say it doesn't take all that, but in my world it did. I was excited about my new vocabulary in the spirit, and I was unashamed about it.

After deliverance from profanity and allowing God to purify my mouth, it was as if the dam was removed and a language broke out. I allowed God to sanctify my words, and put grace on my speech. One day when I was home getting ready for work, I was praying and singing when I heard this loud sound of gibberish. All of a sudden I started sweating and speaking in unknown tongues. I didn't know whether I should laugh or cry. I was like, "What are those?" I didn't recognize my prayer language because my tongues didn't sound like the tongues I heard in church. I made a silent commitment that my prayer language was for the privacy of my home, because surely those tongues couldn't be corporate. I developed an insecurity about my prayer language, so when no one was around, I would be in the house whispering my tongues. Slowly but surely, my prayer language began to build muscle as I developed and increased my communion in privacy. The Holy Spirit took over and began to offer intercession on my behalf with groaning and moaning that I couldn't understand. These encounters would happen over time, and suddenly I developed a kingdom language, and prophetic vocabulary erupted out of my mouth. The Holy Spirit became strong and active like never before. I learned to decree a thing and believed it would be established. As God shifted my language, He ushered me into conversations of Holiness that changed the way I spoke about others as well as myself. I learned to speak well of Him.

Your deliverance is in your mouth. I stopped professing I was gay and began to declare I am a daughter of the King. When my language changed, my identity changed. The progression continued.

APPETITE

Having an appetite can be dangerous if you have no balance control when you eat and over what you eat. I learned that my personality was appetite-driven, and when I ate something I liked, I over indulged. Perversion was connected to my appetite. Darkness had me craving and lusting after the very thing God declared was not good for me. The very thing I was attracted to was the very thing designed to destroy me. The enemy pulled on my appetite and at vulnerable moments after the altar, I found myself being lured by my appetite. Lust is connected to appetite. What you lust for, you go after with a strong intent to not just eat, but over-indulge. The enemy is aware that lust is like a spermatic seed waiting to be released, causing you to become pregnant with sin. You become what you eat. The enemy used my appetite to walk me right into the things that had the ability to kill me. No matter how many times I said I wasn't going to give in to temptation when lust entered my appetite, I opened the refrigerator of sin and ate the very things I craved. Have you ever eaten something until you got full, and when you were done, you were sick, and so stuffed until you fell into depression because you ate what you knew wasn't good for you? That's the vicious cycle I endured after the altar. I feasted upon sexual sin and later regretted it. I then fell into depression, defeat, guilt, shame, and condemnation. I beat myself up and not only listened to the voice of the enemy, but I agreed with him. I cried, called myself stupid, wanted to give up, and felt that this cycle would never end. I would wallow with my head down and would go to God with my heart, my head, and my hands lifted asking for help. I would ask God to change my appetite. I was determined to not suppress sin; I wanted to be delivered. I wanted this same-sex appetite to be removed.

I refused to put my desire on a diet by refusing to ac-knowledge that I wanted it. I didn't want to fake it with God, I wanted deliverance and I wanted it bad. But to be honest, I couldn't shake my desire for the same sex. I couldn't understand how I was at the altar, delivered, yet still craving what I thought was cast out me. Although I was improving and I was able to go weeks and months without falling, I realized it was out of a commitment to God, and not because I didn't want it anymore. I would go boldly to the throne of Grace reminding God that He chose me, that he apprehended me, and I needed His help getting rid of the desires that were not pleasing in His sight. I begged God for help. I didn't want to be in a rehabilitation state in the spirit; I wanted to be totally free.

The more I went to God, the more He would shower me with His love. I couldn't comprehend such a love. How is God loving me, and I'm not faithful, I'm not keeping His commands. The very idea that God loved me through my sinful state moved my heart in ways I can't articulate. I recall rehearsing to God that He's not like man. He's a God of love that can't be described. I would weep before the Lord with a heart full of overwhelming emotions. God would literally rescue me, pick me up, clean me up and clothe me. I refused to hide from God like Adam and Eve did when they sinned in the garden. I refused to stop visiting God in the cool of the day. The love was poured out upon my lips like a woman thirsty and drinking from a well. The Love of God was tangible, visible, and real. My countenance was turned around, and I would arise and feel a sense of victory. Each time I fell, I ran to God and not away from God. It was like God anticipated my arrival, and He would meet me before I could even cry out, " Lord have mercy. " I know many of you reading this book can't comprehend such a love for a homosexual, but I tell you, it was God who delivered me from the pits of evil. I was in the fire after the altar and the Lord stood with me to deliver me.

Let me pause and minister to the one who's walking in condemnation and you feel you can't stop the cravings that cause you to fall. You've been running from God and hiding in shame. Listen! God is awaiting you to deliver you. God loves you and even in your nakedness, there is a special covering He wants to put upon you. Come to the well and drink of the Father's love. You've come too far to quit. You can do it. You will survive, and you will be victorious. Deliverance is your portion. God knows your appetite, and He has plans to make an exchange by replacing your hunger for righteousness where He shall fill you with Himself.

That's exactly what God did for me. God delivered me from the appetite of darkness and gave me a hunger for righteousness. God filled me. My desires became His desires. I tasted of His goodness and after experiencing the love of the Father, I fell in love. I found myself seeking God like an addict craving heroine. God was the source of my appetite, and He filled me until I began to walk in overflow. My taste buds began to change and I was craving prayer, visitation, and the Word. Nothing compared or measured to the love of the Father that quenched my thirst. I began to recognize deliverance when my desires for the same sex were gone. I couldn't believe it. I remember looking at women, and nothing was there. I was empty in my feelings towards the same sex. My gaze was fixed on God and God alone. He became my daily bread, and I took the time to get full off His Word. I promise once you taste of the goodness of Jesus, you won't settle for anything else. Not even sex. God is able to deliver your appetite by giving you Himself. Just taste and see.

The culture of my sexual appetite was dismantled. God didn't just take away the desire, He replaced it with a taste more powerful than anything I've ever tasted. The key to deliverance is to go to the Source of the only one who has the power to set you free. It's not by might, nor by power, but by the Spirit. The focus wasn't on me falling; the focus was on God lifting me up, and saving a wretch like me. Little by little the Lord drove out my enemies.

GOVERNMENT CHANGED

When you are a citizen of a particular country, you are forced to comply with the rules implemented by your government. You are provided a list of policies and procedures, and you are under the structure and confinement of your governmental system in which you reside. Breaking the rules or violating the code can cost you your freedom, as well as your life. Moving to a new country can be difficult, because your life is under the authority of that governmental system. What gives you freedom in one jurisdiction, doesn't give you freedom in another jurisdiction. You have to immediately familiarize yourself with the governmental system before moving or settling to avoid any conflict with the law or the cultural norms.

Even if an American citizen goes to visit another country, it's proper protocol to become aware of the culture to avoid offense. There are certain things that are socially accepted in one country, that are totally unacceptable in another. It's wise to be aware of the governmental system, as well as the culture before relocation.

That's how it was for me after being bound in the homosexual lifestyle for so many years. It was like I was residing in a foreign country where I learned to speak a specific language, have a set appetite, interact with my own kind, and follow the rules of the game. I'd been a part of the homosexual culture for the majority of my life, and I didn't know anything else. I was familiar with the lifestyle and understood everything I needed to know about the life. When I came to Christ, something internal occurred. I recognized something new happened. However, I didn't know what to do with the new found life of Christ. I didn't know the rules, policies, and commitments of the kingdom of God. I didn't understand the principles of the kingdom or the government of God. It was all foreign to me. I had to rediscover the kingdom of God and learn about the government in which I had committed my life to. I had to discover God in a whole new way, and the only way I was able to do that was by submitting myself to the process and adjusting to the new citizenship I committed to after the altar.

I accepted the fact that I had relocated to a new life, and even when I wanted to go back, light overpowered the darkness until it began to shatter. When I would get home sick and attempt to backslide, God would be there to rescue me and bring me back to Himself. I felt like coming to the kingdom of God was like enlisting in an army, and if I attempted to run from the battle, I would be apprehended by God to war until I had the victory. God became Jehovah Gibbor, *the God who wars.* I remember crying and declaring, "I didn't ask for this." God would respond by saying, "But I asked for it. For I knew you before the foundations of the world. I predestined you and called you unto Myself." God refused to let me go back. When I found myself visiting sin, God would rescue me even if He had to snatch me out of the bedchamber. When you come into the kingdom, the battle is no longer yours, but it belongs to the Lord. God will forsake the ninety-nine to come after the one. God dismantled the demonic governmental system by releasing light; which overthrew darkness.

I began to understand the governmental system of the kingdom. The Lord began teaching me about my role in the earth, and why hell hated me and wanted to abort my destiny. The enemy had a plan for my life, and when I came into the earth. He was aware of my destiny. The enemy doesn't play fair, so he began his demonic attack during the most vulnerable times of my life. For many years I grew up in bondage, a slave to homosexuality. The system of homosexuality held me bound. I grew and developed under this system, and witnessed the great bondage of many who entered the lifestyle and felt hopeless. The feeling that you could never be free was overwhelming. The grip was tight, and it appeared unbearable and unbreakable. If there is an indication that freedom is set to come to you, the power of darkness is released to tighten the grip. It takes the power of God to be set free. God had to come and set me free Himself; and that's exactly what He did. Yahweh rescued me from my enemies. When God delivered me from the system of homosexuality, He brought me into His kingdom. God began to train me up in preparation to go back to the very system that held me illegally to release freedom to the captives who are currently held hostage. God delivers, so you can be a deliverer.

Just look at the life of Moses in the book of Exodus. Moses grew up in the home of Pharaoh, the Egyptian King. Moses being a Hebrew was raised under an Egyptian system. He ate what they ate, spoke as they spoke, learned what they learned, and developed as they developed. Moses was delivered from the system he grew up in, and that same system was the one he was assigned to engage, confront, and overthrow. I remember reading how Moses feared going back to the enemy's camp and how he had informed God that he had a stuttering problem. God responded by reminding Moses that He was the God who created Him. Moses' stuttering problem made him feel inadequate about confronting the enemy. Moses didn't feel confident or qualified. That is how I felt when God began giving me assignments early in my deliverance process. I remember telling God that I still looked gay and that I wasn't fit to return because of the residue of sin on my life. I would cry, kick, and scream when God assigned me to any task because I didn't feel saved enough. My impediment was my appearance. God would gently push me to step out and obey assuring me that He was with me. God understood my journey better than me, and it's proven as you continue to read my story.

God was adamant about sending me back to disrupt the very system that had held me bound. My story of redemption was sure to bankrupt hell as many would hear my story and be transformed. I didn't know how God would do it, but so far He was proving that deliverance was the children's bread, and He Was filling me up. The homosexual culture was dismantled, yet I continued to walk with a masculine exterior.

Three

AM I REALLY SAVED?

AM I REALLY SAVED? LIKE FOR REAL, FOR REAL, IN REAL life saved? Those were the questions I pondered day after day during my process post altar. After a year of still looking the same, and not recognizing any physical changes, I would find myself looking in the mirror searching for answers. I couldn't comprehend how nothing was changing externally, and how I was still having cravings for the same sex. In my mind, if deliverance means freedom, why did I still feel bound? What is this bondage? Why am I still having same-sex attractions? What is it God, I questioned over and over. You've stripped me of everything, but nothing is changing. That was my daily conversation with God, yet no immediate answers came. I thought freedom meant I would be free from the very thing that had me bound, so God where are you? I would hold God accountable for finishing what He began in me. I felt that if God truly had plans for my life, He would at least allow me to get an inside scoop on what was going to play out. I was trying to make sense and know God on a level of humanity, and each time I tried to figure out the mind of God concerning me, He would respond, "My thoughts are not your thoughts."

I would attempt to trust God and continue to move forward even when I felt stagnant. One thing I recognized was that my attraction for women was decreasing, and I was winning more battles than I was losing. I began to take on a new sexual diet, where I was able to manage my intake. I remember reading Matthew 5:30, and the day that word became real to me. "If my right hand caused me to sin, cut it off." I knew God didn't mean to literally cut off limbs. However, the things that were designed to pull me into sin were the very things I was to cut off, remove, and separate myself from. I tried to cut off the attraction, but the harder I tried, the harder it became. Then the Lord reminded me, Sophia it's not by might, nor by power, but by my Spirit. I began to weep as I fully entrusted my entire life and process with the God who chose me and apprehended me.

One my greatest attributes was my honesty, transparency and brokenness before the Father. I didn't hide what I was feeling and always presented Him with my struggles. If I was to be real, there was still something there. I refused not to acknowledge the hidden desires that were trying to hide and lie dormant.

I didn't want my demons to sleep; I wanted to be free. I wanted to be free and there was no way I would be out of the closet as a homosexual, only to hide in the closet as a believer. I had to confront what was confronting me. I knew that if I got weak, I could go backward by falling into sexual sin with the same sex, so I engaged in war by exposing my weakness to God. My desire was to be sure I was delivered and not suppressing sin due to my loyalty and commitment to God. I wanted freedom. I wanted to be sure that the very taste of sin would be removed from my life. I didn't want to depend on my strength. I wanted to depend on God. During the journey, I fell, but the falls were decreasing as my relationship with God increased.

I couldn't put my finger on what the triggers were for my relapses. I was still very much masculine, and it seemed as if God was unbothered by my external appearance. He was working internally, my character was shifting, my heart was changing, and I was feeling freedom on the inside, yet I couldn't shake how I felt defeated when I looked at myself in the mirror. To be perfectly honest, I would have had a fit if God would have touched my identity because I had no clue about who I was outside of the exterior I'd grown to love, embrace, and know. I gave Him permission and access to touch my entire life, but silently prayed, "Please Lord allow me to love you just the way I am." I had a fear of undressing physically and tapping into the realm of nakedness where I would have to address the real me. I had been hiding from Sophia for so long; I don't think I could handle the sight of her. I say her because for years I lived in a state of deception where I put on a role of masculinity, believing that I was a man. I stubbornly fought God and declared, "You can convert my heart, but don't you dare convert my appearance."

I couldn't comprehend how I was refusing to allow God to change my appearance while this was the very enemy that was tormenting me. I was begging for freedom with a closed fist on my process. The very things I was once proud of, I was becoming ashamed of. There was a time when I enjoyed being called sir, dude, or bruh. It was even more flattering when women hit on me. However, over time, I found myself becoming offended when women would hit on me. I couldn't understand why I was being approached by women when I was openly acknowledging I was saved and I didn't get down with the lifestyle anymore. "Don't they know I'm saved," I would whisper to myself. It was difficult because my image wasn't articulating what my heart was declaring. This became a constant battle for me as I walked through my deliverance process. My residue was attracting and speaking that the door of perversion was cracked open, and if the right opportunity presented itself, I would fall. So it wasn't a matter of not being free, the issue was that the residue was attracting darkness. Where there was residue, the enemy had a badge of false authority, utilizing his license to arrest me at will. The blood of Jesus was my way of escape out of the temporary holding cell I found myself in from time to time.

The residue on my life was creating a whirlwind of problems. Due to the residue on my life, I found myself spending more time defending my freedom rather than walking in it. Many people would pressure and burden me with statements like, "I thought you were saved, why you still dress like that? Why won't you put on a skirt?" The pressure was unbearable. Making adjustments by trying to balance my new embrace of God and their view of what deliverance looked like was overwhelming. Many people in church were pressuring me to change my apparel, and made comments like, "I wonder what Sophia would look like in a dress." I would get instantly offended, humiliated, and outraged. It wasn't even a thought of what I would look like. Church folks were attempting to rush my process, due to their inability to discern where I was in the spirit. God was driving my demons out little by little, yet the pressure released by outsiders almost aborted my process. God moved in each time, personally rescuing me and reminding me that this battle is not mine but belonged to Him. I would cry out to God, asking that He reveal my heart, show what I'm doing in secret, share with them how I arise at 4 a.m. seeking your face; how I study for hours, and how I'm fasting and crying out. Yet the Lord would declare that what I was doing in secret was being set up for a public reward. In the midst of persecution, I would continue to put my trust in God and allow Him to complete the work. The pressure pushed me closer to the Father, who proved He would never fail me.

Prophetic Gone Wrong

Early in my process, I remember attending a service and a well-known, powerful prophet was in town from Africa. Many people kept saying I should attend the service, due to the accuracy of the prophet. I was excited yet nervous at the same time because I wasn't sure what to expect. I just knew God had something good to say about me, especially because of my new walk with Him, and how much I was progressing. So I went to the service, sat in the front, and witnessed the prophet go forth. I was dressed in a Kobe Bryant Laker's jersey, jean shorts, Air Force Ones, and my hair was faded. I had on Joop cologne and was feeling fresh. I was ready to hear the Word of the Lord. This prophet was prophesying and going forth in the service and began to prophesy as many fell out and shouted as he released word after word.

The atmosphere was intense, my hands slightly lifted, as I shifted closer to the edge of my seat, contemplating going to the altar. My heart began to beat, and my nose broke out in a sweat, as I jumped up from my seat and made my way to the altar waiting to hear the word God had for me. Immediately the prophet anointed my head with oil, and began to speak over my life. I felt the pressure of his hands on my head, yet the words coming out of his mouth couldn't possibly be for me. There is no way God was saying these words about me. At this moment I attempted to block out the words spoken, so I shut my eyes and rejected every word that proceeded from his mouth. He shouted, "Man of God," as he prophesied over my life as if I was a man. I couldn't believe it. I began to wonder if God had abandoned me, or if it was my portion to be shamed publicly. I was caught between two worlds. I was too far gone from the homosexual community to return to the vomit God was removing me from, and too close to God to turn back on His faithfulness. I felt stuck in the middle of a decision with no clue on which way to turn. Immediately after service, I found myself rushing home to throw myself on my restroom floor with the desire…Kill me now God.

The restroom instantly became pitch black as a spirit of suicide boldly approached me. This spirit spoke death, and left me without options other than end your life now. The words were loud, stern and powerful. I was being lured with the idea that life would be better if I didn't exist. In the midst of a total blackout, right before my eyes, hell played out a vision of God abandoning me, shaming me, and mocking me. I jumped off the floor, disarrayed and fatigued as I turned on water in an attempt to silence the voice, but nothing could drown out the strength of this voice declaring, "Just die Sophia, just die." I then reached for the radio that was in my window seal, to turn on the music so no one would hear me cry out for death. I hated my life, I regretted the process, and the only way out was death. It was too much pressure, and I couldn't handle it. The torment was real! There were days I felt like ghetto boys, "My mind playing tricks on me." The torment was so real; it was beginning to make me question my salvation, my life, and God. I was becoming paranoid and spent hours wondering if I was still gay, worried about what others were saying about me, and simply being overwhelmed with what God was doing through me. I stretched out on the floor, snot running down my nose, tears pouring down my cheeks, fist pounding the floor, screaming for help.

The entire time, the enemy spoke in my ear agreeing that death would be the best solution for me. His words intensified as he confirmed my thoughts that ever since I got saved, life had gotten worse. The crazy part is that he didn't tell me to return to homosexuality. The enemy truly convinced me that death was the best answer. I wondered how I could just put an end to this life. What was my plan of death, and how could I execute my plan? Then immediately something shifted on the inside of me like an alarm clock going off, and I refused to hit the snooze button. The alert caught my attention, as the Lord declared, "Sophia I will never leave you or forsake you. I am going to use your story. I have plans for your life, for I know the plans I have for you daughter. Plans to prosper you, and bring you to an expected end."

As the words of God pierced my heart, my body rested on the floor in total desperation and brokenness. The Lord began to teach me about renewing my mind and how understanding His supernatural power was far deeper than my fragile intellect.

My emotions were all over the place, as I spent my days crying and broken before the Lord. The more broken I became, the more God spoke. "The flesh is weak, but the spirit is willing." Days would go by, no food, no drink, simply a broken soul poured out at the feet of Jesus, seeking Help. I felt helpless, but I kept pushing. Something on the inside of me was thrusting me forward. Supernatural encounters would break out, and I was tapping realms of accessing the voice of God more clearly. I would hear God awaken me with words of beauty, calling me beautiful, beloved, and daughter. These words were new, and words I had never thought about myself. I would respond am I beautiful? Am I your beloved? Am I a daughter? At this moment, I needed such confirmation to affirm, validate, and endorse me with words from my Father. I swallowed these words, and it was sweet as honey. The more God affirmed me, the more I believed every word that proceeded from His mouth. I was becoming vulnerable internally, and all guards were dropped as I embraced the love of a Father. My heart was bowed to the ground, and I cried out "Not my will, but let thy will be done." I began to progress internally from that moment on. There was a supernatural advancement in my heart, and the walls fell as God went to the root to uproot the words that were planted years ago. God began to pull from the root and dismantled word curses like you have false identity, you a little man, dyke, butch, lesbo, homo, and every word connected to the stronghold of deception, rejection and trauma. The words of the Lord shattered the very forces of false words rooted in my life. God began to dismantle by pulling apart every system that kept me connected to the origin of homosexuality. After uprooting the demonic words, God began to water my life like a gardener who waters their garden in anticipation of producing fruit. God watered me with His Word. He spent time tending to my life by plucking away weeds, and planting His seed. I was beginning to bear fruit. The fruit of the Spirit was alive and active.

Suddenly I began to get uncomfortable in my own skin. I wanted to rip off my flesh layer by layer, and be released from my own skin. Like a bird being trapped in a sealed cage, desiring to be free, I began to feel like a shell was over me, and like an eagle, I was ready to hatch. The grip was tight, but the more I yielded to God, the lighter the grip became. I knew that my freedom was in God, and the blood was my access to freedom. So I stayed close to the Deliverer, who had the authority to completely deliver me. I asked God to make me His blueprint by showing me what He saw that I didn't see. Because I understood that His thoughts were not my thoughts, I totally surrendered and gave God access to the areas I once refused to give Him access to.

The first thing God came for was my declarations of "I'll never." And this is where the journey of my external feminine progression began. Over the years I decreed some "I'll nevers" and I held strongly to my proclamations. As a masculine stud our street code was to be upheld and honored because our reputation was on the line. In the homosexual community, there were specific protocols, and certain things we wouldn't do like, never wear a skirt, never wear makeup, never wear nails, never wear heels, never wear panties or a bra, and most of all, never date a man. I mean you name it, I said it. I stood on these codes as if it was my Bible. I created worlds with my words, which gave the enemy access to bind me by the words I spoke. God reversed the very curse I spoke over my own life. Let's see how these I'll never's play out, as you continue to read.

Four

Joke Gone Right

IF ANYONE KNOWS ME, THEY KNOW THAT I LOVE A GOOD joke. I enjoy cracking on other people, laughing, and simply having fun. I would find a joke out of any situation, to get a good laugh. Sometimes those jokes turned on me, and became a joke gone right instead of wrong. You remember reading how it was a joke the first time I attended church, and Lord did God take advantage of the moment by arresting me on that day and calling me to Himself. As I look back over those years, I laugh and discover a side of God that's amazing. I can recall going to church as a joke on that Sunday morning then bam, God took my breath away, and apprehended my entire soul. What a cool God we serve. Don't be so deep people; even God has a sense of humor. There is fullness of joy and laughter in His presence. I love how God mysteriously worked miracles through my life, by seizing the most unique moments to set me free.

Many of you often wonder, how does a stud transform externally? You wonder if they just put on some clothes and a little make-up to prove they are delivered or do they follow a specific blueprint towards regaining their beauty for ashes. Heck, I used to wonder how studs go from being masculine to feminine as well? I sure didn't think I would be the person writing this book, sharing with you how God did it for me. So you don't get it twisted, feminine is not simply changing clothes, putting on lipstick, and switching. If that was the case, we wouldn't have lipstick lesbians, the girly girls who are in the closet and not suspected due to their exterior being feminine. However, I want to share my journey and how God advanced my femininity progressively. I didn't simply change clothes; I changed my life. Who I am today didn't take a year, it took time for me to be reset and return to the original state in which God created me to be. Everyone's journey is different, this is my story, so let me share how God took a joke, and turned it into so much more.

Mother's Day Prank

Mother's Day was approaching, and I was wondering what I could possibly get my mother. I was living in Mount Vernon, IL, and my mother was in Chicago, which was three hours away. As I pondered over and over what to get my mom, I thought to myself, "Wow, I will be my mom's present." My mother usually asked for a "box" which meant she wanted gifts inside, so what better gift than to show up as that box for Mother's Day. I went into prank mode, and shared with my friend Devon that I wanted to be a girl for Mother's Day. Devon laughed and said you are a girl silly. I said, "No, a real girl, like a girly girl." Devon laughed and said, "Okay, let's go shopping." I took a deep swallow, sweat broke out on my nose, and immediately I felt shame. I didn't know how I could go shopping and try on girl clothes when I was as masculine as they came. It just didn't look or feel right. At this point, my hair had grown out, and I had corn-rows, my pants were still baggy, and I was still very masculine. Devon told me to calm down and not to worry, because she would handle all of the preliminaries. I quickly called my sister and my brother-in-law advising them of the joke that was brewing. They were excited and proceeded to pump me up. We worked out the details of the joke, and decided that I would show up at church to surprise my mother.

Devon and I went to the mall to shop for an outfit. While shopping, I was embarrassed because we were in the women's section, and nothing stood out. We were in Maurice's and at that time they had a women and men's section, so i walked to the men's section while Devon shopped for my outfit. I was pretending to be looking for something in the men's section to play it off, however I was nervous about this joke, and kept saying to myself, "Lord this is for my mom, and as soon as this is over, I'm going back to the norm." I couldn't wait to get the joke out of the way, so I kept my mom's face in my view whenever I wanted to say forget it and give up on the prank. It was my heart to surprise my mom as a girly girl, since she had spent over a decade looking at her little girl lost in masculinity. Although she loved me through my mess, she really missed her baby girl, and I knew it, but I was too far gone in my manhood to change. As Devon shopped she was all smiles and having the time of her life, while I waddled in the men's section looking crazy and confused. My two braids were nappy and in need of a touchup, but I was just waiting it out. As we shopped I prayed that we wouldn't run into anyone, however the entire time all I kept hearing was, "Hey Sophia," as people I knew came in and out of the store. I was like, " Oh hey y'all, as I really pretended to be looking for something." Devon would raise up outfits asking how I liked what she had picked out, and I would shrug my shoulders like, "Girl I don't care what you get, this isn't for me, this for my momma." I would follow up with, "You just better not pick up a skirt."

Once Devon picked the outfit, we both went into the dressing room. I was so ashamed because I didn't want anyone to see me dressed in girl's clothing. To me, I looked like some sort of drag queen. I hated the entire shopping process, and I kept saying, " I quit, this ain't me bruh." But once again my mother would show before my face, and I would be reminded that it wasn't about me; it was about my mother. Devon picked some brown striped Capri pants, a yellow feminine fitted blouse, and because I refused any other shoe, a flip-flop to seal the deal. To the fitting room we went, as I tried on my new soon to be garments.

In the fitting room, Devon stood outside the door as she handed me one item at a time. I tried on each of the items with my back turned from the mirror, and my eyes closed. I refused to look at myself. I was fixed on the idea that it didn't matter what I looked like because it was not about me. Once Devon approved that I could fit the outfit and all was well, she purchased everything. She then carried the bags out of the store, and took me to get jewelry, underwear, and a bra. Funny, right? Here we are headed to the women's section to pick out undergarments. You talking about embarrassed. I was content on wearing some boxers and a sports bra, but was advised that I better not do such a thing. This joke was beginning to overwhelm me. I had no clue what my bra or underwear sizes were. I was out of the loop regarding anything that pertained to my femininity.

Devon was graced for the assignment, as she patiently assisted me in this process. She didn't laugh or make me feel weird. She was literally like an angel in disguise. With everything all picked out and ready to go, we walked through the mall to leave. Devon turned and looked at my hair, which was in two French braids, and said, "Hey, I have an idea." I looked out the corner of my eye with a look of, "I'm done, this is it." Devon said, "Let's go to the beauty shop and see if you can get your hair flat ironed." "Ummm, how about not!" After much convincing off we went to the beauty shop. The ride was about a mile. However it felt like a lifetime as I complained the entire ride saying, "I'm not going inside if people are there. I'm not wearing my hair down, and on and on I vented. Devon continued to drive, not saying a word.

We pull up at Charisma's Shop located in the center of

downtown Mt. Vernon. I'm saying downtown, but to be honest it's a small little city with about three stores, a courthouse, and a church. Devon smiled and sang, "We're here." My eyes roll to the back of my head as I think to myself, "What's next?" Devon goes ahead of me, walks inside the shop, assesses the atmosphere and makes an appointment for me. My heart pounds as I wait in the car, praying that everything goes wrong, but unfortunately everything was going right. Devon taps on the window and says, "Come on Sophia, no one is inside, and Bre is ready for you." I stagger out of the car, cursing silently in my head as I walk inside. Bre closes the blinds, locks the door, and begins to style my hair. She unravels the braids, and gently begins to comb through the nappy roots while smiling and saying, "It's going to be so cute, Sophia." "Gross," is what I thought! How can this be cute? Heck, I don't want to be cute, I'm good the way I am. My body complied and I relaxed as I turned over my will to a power that was stronger than mine.

Something came over me, and I began to trust the process as Devon cheered me on, and Bre worked her magic. The entire process, I requested not to be turned towards the mirror, and I refused to look the style even after she was finished. I put my hands over my eyes to ensure I didn't get a glimpse of my new look. If I could have performed the prank blindfolded, that would have been wonderful. Devon kept saying that my hair was long and it was thick, but I didn't care, I felt weird having hair hitting the back of my neck. I wanted to yank that hair in a ponytail and walk away.

Bre wrapped my hair up, and put a scarf on my head. As she finished my hair, I sank into the chair, and wondered to myself, "How in the world did I end up here? How did I set myself up for such a disaster." I kept saying, "My mom is going to be so happy, so it's all worth it." Something internal was trying to relax and soften me, yet there was a resistance as I fought what I was feeling externally. I didn't know how the joke would end, but I was excited to see my mother smile.

4 A.M. TRAIN RIDE

After I arrived home from my day of shopping, getting my hair done, and doing this whole girly makeover, I packed my clothes inside my gym bag and prepared for my trip to Chicago. Inside my gym bag was my one girly outfit, the underwear, bra, and of course my Jordan's, Timberland boots, gym shorts, and baggy jeans. I had it in my mind that Sunday morning I would dress in my feminine garments, and as soon as church was over go back to the norm. I couldn't wait to get this over with. I called my sister and made sure she had everything set for my arrival. I checked my train's status, and I was set to head north for Mother's Day. I called my mother and told her that her Mother's Day box would be issued by my sister on Sunday after church. Boy oh Boy was she excited. She loves getting boxes because she always looks forward to getting some extra cash from her children. Little did she know, I was the box, and although I wasn't thrilled, it would be her greatest gift, and that's all that mattered.

Chooooo Chooooo! Amtrak pulls up, and here I am

climbing the stairs to jump on the muggy, musty, train filled with all types of people. I remember saying to myself, "Sophia are you sure you want to do this?" As I gazed around, I reflected on how good my mom had been towards me, and thought, " It's a sacrifice I must make." My mother was the motivating factor the entire trip. My heart pounced, and I kept trying to imagine the moment, but I kept drawing a blank. I couldn't even picture or imagine what I would look like. I was so far gone that my perception of me as a woman was faded away. I drifted off into a deep sleep, and before I knew it, "Homewood is your next stop." I grabbed my gym bag and headed to meet my sister and brother-in-law.

I greeted my sister and brother-in-law, and we were all super excited about the "big reveal." Although I was nervous, anxious, and unsure of the results, I was still excited about the surprise. I was dropped off at Betty Mo's house, and the plan was for me to get dressed at her home so everyone would be surprised to see me. I arrived at Betty's house, and she was so happy to see me. She welcomed me into her home with open arms and informed me that I had access to the rooms upstairs. She told me to take all the time I needed, but that I needed to be downstairs by 10:45 a.m. I smiled and replied, "Okay." Betty and my mother were close friends and were in the choir together. Betty knew about my lifestyle and gender confusion, but she never mumbled a word.

Upstairs I went as the wooden floors creaked with every step I took. I felt like I was entering a horror movie as I made my way to the bedroom. I threw my gym bag down, and sat on the bed thinking about this joke over and over in my head. Finally, I jumped up, showered and prepared myself to get ready for church. I began to pull each item out of my bag, dreading the process as I picked up the capris and prepared to crease them. Weird, eyes rolling in the back of my head trying to figure out how I went from ironing Enyce jeans to some capris pants. Next out the bag was this bright tight-fitted yellow shirt, and once again, I'm staring at this stuff like, "Who putting this on?" Funny now but trust me, this felt weird on every level. Once I finished ironing, I laid my clothes on the bed and prepared to get dressed. I walked through the room huffing and puffing like the Hulk. I got dressed in a mirrorless room, and I didn't have a clue about what I looked like. I took the comb, stood in front of a blank wall, and began to comb my wrap down. I then sat on the bed. I was unaware of what I looked like, but I knew I felt different. In my mind, I kept the focus on the surprise being for my mom, and not for me. I called Devon and shared with her that I was dressed and ready to head out. Devon had a sound of pure joy as she excitedly asked, "How do you look?" I responded, " I don't have a clue, I got dressed without looking." Devon then stated, "You got this Sophia, you look pretty." I sarcastically replied, "Sure."

THE REVEAL

"Sophia, are you ready? Sophia, it's 10:45," Betty yelled from downstairs. I jumped off the bed with an attitude, eyes rolling, and a few huffs and puffs. I was talking to Devon as I headed out of the bedroom, sharing with her that I couldn't wait to get this over with. Then this happened. I ran into a mirror that was in the hallway on my way down the stairs. I crashed into myself by accident, and immediately it felt like a fatal crash with destiny as I hit the floor with tears strolling beautifully down my cheeks. I cried and couldn't stop crying. Something broke inside of me, and I couldn't resist the tears. Devon was on the phone, asking, "Sophia, are you okay? Sophia are you there?" I cried out, "Oh my gosh Devon, this is me. I look so beautiful. Wow, look at me." I hung up the phone and walked closer to the mirror, making closer contact with what I was seeing in front of me. Rubbing my hands down the mirror, I patted myself down, as I wondered if this was a dream. Immediately I heard the voice of God declare, "Look at my beloved, in whom I'm well pleased. My daughter, in my image, after my likeness. My Sophia Ruffin, oh how beautiful you are to behold, for today I give you beauty for ashes. My butterfly can now soar." I was undone as I wept bitterly with tears of joy, excitement, and uncertainty. I could have lingered at that moment for hours, but Betty was calling my name. I couldn't move a muscle. I was too stunned. I got up and walked down the stairs, and Betty began to cry, and continued to say, "Your mom is going to be so happy Sophia. Oh, how beautiful you are young lady." We walked out the door, jumped in her van, and headed to service. My heart pounded with anxiety and excitement.

Surprise Momma
(I love me some Doris Hodo - Ruffin)

I finally arrived at the church, and I walked inside and waited by the sanctuary door, awaiting the ushers with the white gloves to escort me to my seat. The choir was on the stand, and the first person I recognized was my momma. I was escorted to a seat next to my sister, my niece and two nephews. They hugged me and couldn't stop saying "Auntie you're so beautiful." Auntie, look at you. They were touching my face, and kissing my cheeks. My sister grabbed my hand and held it with a look of admiration and security. My brother-in-law looked over, nodded his head and smiled as he played the keyboard. My oldest nephew, who was on the drums, gave me a big smile as he lip-synced "You look beautiful auntie." What a powerful moment. My family rejoiced as if I was raised from the dead. Funny how I'm using such an analogy because that's exactly what it felt like.

My mother observed all the commotion, so she looked over at her friend Betty, with a face of confusion as she looked over her glasses, and asked her friend, "Who is that with my family?" Her lips were mumbling, but I couldn't make out the words as she shrugged her shoulders. She continued to ask, "Who is that lady with my family, and what is she doing?" What's all the commotion about? My mother was clueless. She stared at me with a look of mystery, and continued to attempt to sing with the choir, yet she was so distracted. I couldn't believe my mother didn't know who I was. I looked at her and smiled, waiting for her to get excited and wave, but she had no clue who I was.

Finally, Betty said, "Doris that's your daughter." My mother covered her mouth, her eyes enlarged, and she stood with her arms reaching for a hug. It was like her breath was taken, as she prepared for such an embrace. The pastor halted the service and allowed us to have our moment. I ran into my mother's arms, and she wept over me. Her heart was relieved, and she continued to say, "Baby, my baby, Sophia, you are so beautiful. My baby, my baby. " That moment was one of the most powerful mother-daughter encounters I ever experienced. We hugged and cried, and enjoyed the moment. The very fact that my mother saw no residue and couldn't recognize her own child was a clear indication that my deliverance was full term.

At the end of service, we went home, and everyone talked about that moment. I was so happy to be part of bringing my mother so much joy. When it was time to undress, I tried to put on my clothes that were in my gym bag, and I couldn't fit them. I couldn't put them on. It was so weird, as I kept trying to put on the other clothes in my bag. I had no power to put any of those garments on. I didn't know what to do and had no clue what was happening. I called Devon and shared what was taking place. I shared that I couldn't put on the clothes in the bag, and questioned what I should do. I began to ask God what I was going to do. The Lord spoke and said that my garments had changed, and He had given me beauty for ashes. Old things were passed away and everything from this day forward was new. I wept and wept. I felt a ripping in my soul. I was stripped from the lifestyle of homosexuality and the residue. The spirit completely lost its grip and let me go. I wore the same outfit for three days until I made it back to Mt. Vernon. When I arrived back home, Devon had seven feminine outfits for me, and over time my wardrobe was made new. I eventually got rid of all my clothing, and God gave me new garments. Being that I wasn't sure what type of clothes to wear, I found myself trying to find my own personal style.

My exterior had completely shifted, and I was becoming familiar with the new me. I didn't know what was next. I was moving into a realm where I was unfamiliar with myself and had to place total dependency on God. Once my exterior progressed and the residue was dismantled, a new level of freedom was released. Over time, along the journey of my new found progression, God began to overthrow my "I'll never" declarations.

Five

∞

The Tale of I'll Never

Have you ever heard the saying, "Never say never?" We'll I am a firm believer in this statement, because the very things I boldly declared would never happen in my life, guess what? It all happened. I can recall many days and nights I would blurt out, "Oh I'll never do that." I had no idea that these "I nevers" would become my reality. Let me take you on a few of these "I'll never" journeys and show you how the things I refused became the things I embraced. Many people have asked me if I transformed easily. As you read in Chapter 4, transformation was not something done intentionally. It was a prank that went right. It was God's ordained moment to bring restoration and progression to my identity. God never showed me the full picture of who I would become, and to be honest I am still progressing. This walk has become blind faith, where I yield to the process and trust God with giving me beauty for ashes. I don't connect putting on a dress, skirt or makeup with deliverance. However this is my story on how I journeyed out of masculinity into my femininity with comfort. Whether with a skirt, jeans, heels or sneakers, I discovered internal and external beauty.

I'll Never Wear Girl Clothes

Welp, as you can see, that bubble burst in Chapter 4. I believe God has a sense of humor because only God could pull off a prank so right. This is why I love God so much. He does all things with grace, love, and beauty. Right now, let me do a praise break and #Pop #Pop #Pop in the spirit realm on the enemy that's been blasting on me. Many people view God as a deity, but I have learned to view God as my Father. He handled my fragile spirit with care, as He walked me through a journey of transformation, and gave me double honor in place of my shame. When I made the declarations, "I'll never" it was bold, loud, and carried weight. I am a firm believer that God watches over His word to perform it, and if He spoke a thing in my life before the foundation of the world, no devil in hell could curse it. Not even me. God is a good, good Father, and if you are reading this book and trying to figure out how your story will end, heed my advice, "Keep soaring, keep living, keep progressing, and allow God to transform you in his timing." The journey of deliverance I'm on is going from glory to glory as I have learned to trust God with my entire life.

Before there was an external manifestation of deliverance, God dealt with me internally. He cleaned me up from the inside out, getting rid of all demonic mold that had been affecting my system. God removed all the filth around my heart, tore down demonic strongholds, and purified the very being of my identity. God softened my heart, which eventually caused the very nature of my identity to be softened. So know that God has the ability to take your, "I never" and use it for His glory. Let's take a look at each level of progression. Please know that my transformation was not instantaneous, but progressive.

I'll Never Wear A Skirt

The funniest I'll never declaration was when I would shout loudly, "I will never wear a skirt." I was comfortable in capris pants, jeans, and dress pants, but oh no, ain't nobody putting on a skirt. I refused to wear skirts, and each time someone would say they wonder what I would look like in one, I would smirk and say, "I guess you'll never know, so use your imagination." Little did I know, one day, in summer of 2008, I had this yearning to dress up for a conference. I couldn't shake it. I pictured myself in all long white, beautiful skirt and turquoise jewelry. I had the outfit in my head and laughed at myself because I had no idea why I wanted to wear this particular look. I saw the entire picture from head to toe. I wanted to flat iron my hair, polish my nails and toes, and dress up. I thought I was losing my mind, but the image became stronger and clearer. At this point, I was comfortable in my girly outfits; I just wasn't wearing a skirt. I don't know if it was because I was uncomfortable, or just afraid to show my legs. I was determined to find the skirt I envisioned, and with a sense of peace, I was excited about getting dressed.

I recall going shopping, and as soon as I walked inside of Maurice's the first thing I saw was a long, flair out white skirt, with a white shirt. I was like, "Wow that's it. That's the outfit I saw in my head." The mannequin even had on silver and turquoise jewelry. Without thinking, and without trying it on, I grabbed the outfit, and purchased it. During this part of my process I was more comfortable shopping for myself, however I still used Devon and my sister Alison for help. This process wasn't easy, but I yielded to the Holy Spirit, and walked it out. The night of the event, I got my nails and toes done. I got a basic manicure and pedicure with a design on the big toe. I got dressed, putting on the skirt for the first time, and OMG I looked amazing. I felt so light and free. I could feel the breath of God upon me, dressing me, with each garment I put on. I felt so clean and pure, a feeling like none other. I combed my wrap down, allowing my hair to flow. I put on my jewelry, and off to church, I went. Everyone was looking and gazing upon me in awe, as they witnessed another level of transformation upon my life. I was excited about how beautiful and natural it felt to put on the outfit God had designed and picked out just for me. During my first encounter with dressing feminine, Devon dressed me, but this time it was all God. God put the look in my head and executed the look perfectly. I can recall feeling a sense of freedom, as the stronghold of "I'll never" was destroyed.

I want you to know that me putting on a skirt didn't confirm my deliverance, the blood of Jesus confirmed it. Me putting on a skirt was a level of progression towards my femininity. I want to prophesy to you, that if you obey God, He will dress you. He has the perfect garments in mind just for you. It wasn't man's timing; it was God's perfect timing. Skirts aren't my favorite things to wear, however, the power of "I'll never" lost its grip, and I became open to embracing all levels of my femininity, internally, and externally.

I'll Never Wear Heels

Now I'm sure you all are wondering what type of shoes I had been wearing with my capris pants and skirts? I thought you would never ask. Well, Old Navy was my favorite store and still is, to be honest. I literally owned every color flip-flop in the store. I would rack up in season and out of season because I refused to put on a baby doll shoe or a heel. I couldn't imagine walking in a high heel shoe. I just knew I would fall over and break my neck. I was a Jordan, Combat Boot, Flip Flop type woman, and to this day, I'm still a sneaker head. Baby doll shoes and heels were out of the question. I would be dressed so beautifully from the neck to the knee, and once you got to the feet, I would have on a flip-flop. I didn't care how bad it looked; I just knew I wasn't wearing anything with a bulk under my foot.

One day I was walking through Target when I randomly walked past a pair of black heels. I grabbed the heel and said to myself, "This a nice shoe." Not giving it much thought, I decided to try the heel on to see if I could walk in it. I remember calling for Devon to come over to the shoe section, so I could show her how I was walking in the heel. We both cracked up laughing, as she said, "Sophia I think you can walk in those girl." I laughed and kept saying, "They feel nice." After much debate, I purchased my first pair of heels. I put my dress on, put on my short black heels, held my head up, and felt tall. No one warned me to never walk in the grass with heels. I walked through the grass, and my heels drove deep into the ground as I stumbled and lost balance almost hitting the ground. I played it off real good, pretending like I was okay when deep down I was thinking, "Oh Lord." After my first heel experience, I can now say that heels have been added to my shoe collection. I am still very versatile in my shoe wear. However my shoe game has progressed. The "I'll never wear heels" was destroyed.

I'll Never Wear Make-up

Carmex and lip balm were my favorite go to make-up items. I wouldn't leave home without something smooth to rub on my lips. Carmex became my lip for the day. I can recall one day being introduced to Bath and Body Works shiny lip gloss. I immediately became addicted to this gloss. I would shine up my lips, put water on my eyebrows to slick them down, rub lotion on my face, and boom, I was made up for the day. Bare face on fleek! I found myself admiring women who knew how to beat their face. However, the closest I was getting to a beat face was lotion, gloss, and water. Don't get me wrong; there is nothing wrong with a natural face with no make-up, however, in this chapter, I want to demonstrate the progression I made in this area of my life. Many of you might say, "You don't have to wear makeup to be feminine." And you are absolutely right, but the point I want to highlight is how make-up was a progressive step in my walk.

One day I was home visiting my family in Chicago. My sister was in the restroom putting on make-up and getting dolled up for the evening. I sat in there admiring her and staring as she applied each product to her face. She would always ask to put some mascara on my lashes or to apply some eyeshadow to my eyes. I would immediately respond, "No way, I'm never wearing make-up." I would go on and on about how I didn't need it and didn't want it. She would look at me and say, "Sis I just want to try some shadow on you." I would laugh, leave the restroom and scream, "Nope." Then one day, out of the clear blue, I said, " You know what, go ahead sis, put some eyeshadow on me." She laughed, smiled, and quickly went through her makeup bag looking for the right colors that would pop on my complexion. She reached for purples and browns and then began the process of shaping my brows and applying eyeshadow. I held my breath, closed my eyes, and trusted her with my face. With my eyes shut, I could feel her smiling as she applied some basic make-up to my face. When she finished, I glanced in the mirror and thought, "Wow Soph, you cute." That was the beginning of me stepping into another level of progression. I was ready to play in makeup.

When I arrived back to my house, I wanted to begin putting eye shadow on and getting my brows done. I made regular visits to JC Penney's salon and allowed them to arch my eyebrows. I then started shopping in the make-up section looking for different kinds of eyeshadows to apply. I didn't have a clue how to put it on, or what colors I needed to blend with what. To be honest, I still don't have a clue, but I continue to try. There was a time I applied blush to my eyes thinking it was shadow. Yeah, I give you permission to laugh. I looked like a clown, but I kept trying. When I found a color that worked, I stayed with that color through every season. I enjoyed playing in make-up. My make-up game increased over the years, and I learned to apply it. I even became skilled enough to apply it to others.

The make-up didn't define my femininity; it enhanced it. I want you to know that it's not the make-up that's the focus. It's the fact that everything I declared I would never do, are the very things I do, and it was another level of progression I made.

I'll Never Date a Man

I was under the impression that when God delivered me, I would be single all of my life. I just knew there was no future in me dating. I wasn't attracted to men, and I didn't see myself dating a man. I was content with being single and saved. I didn't even know I had an attraction to men. I didn't leave the altar and suddenly have eyes, ears, feelings, and desires for a man. I believed that I would be delivered from same-sex attraction, but I didn't believe I could have any form of attraction for a man. I refused to jump into a heterosexual relationship in the hope that this would remove homosexual desires. I would say over and over, "I'm not gay, but I don't want a man." I couldn't imagine myself finding a man attractive to the point of me desiring any form of intimacy.

Men were far from my desire, until one day I saw this guy, and immediately sirens went off. My eyes were opened to an attraction I never imagined. I looked at this brother over and over, and said to myself, "He's cute. He's fly. He's attractive, and I dig his style. I laughed out loud at myself, and wondered, "Who am I?" Where did this sudden attraction come from? I shook my head no, while everything in me said, "Yes." It was as if God had ripped the scales off of my eyes, and allowed me to see from a different perspective. I was beginning to view men in a different light. The lack of trust and anger I had towards men collapsed, and I was able to see the heart of a man. I would look at men and could literally see myself dating a man. I desired to be embraced by the masculinity of a man. I was in awe of God. I didn't prepare or force the attraction. It was a supernatural awakening. As God was giving me my identity back, He was restoring my sight towards the opposite sex. I didn't lust and long for them. I embraced a level of progression where I went from no attraction to a full awareness and attraction that God purified my view towards men. Another "I'll never" was destroyed as I progressed in another area of my femininity.

I wanted to share these snippets of my "I'll nevers" to demonstrate how God will take the very things you declare you will never do to better you. By themselves changing your clothes, shoes, make-up, hair, and dating the opposite sex does not prove deliverance nor make one more feminine. But I am sharing my journey down the road to deliverance and how God walked me out of masculinity. My sexuality wasn't the only area I needed deliverance; my entire being needed Him. The macho, manly, strong, and aggressiveness was removed as I learned to embrace being womanly and more ladylike. Although these are external manifestations, in this process I discovered my heart, appearance, and character developed a level of sensitivity and gentleness. I learned to disassociate from the things that fueled masculinity, and embraced new areas of my womanhood.

The greatest aspect of my process was that God fueled every area of my identity. I didn't attempt to dress up, change my appearance based on the opinion of others, or convince myself I was completely free. God was involved in each intimate detail of my deliverance. Each moment, each step, was a new chapter in my story of deliverance. Like a husband diligently providing for his bride to be, God covered me with His undying love. He nourished and dressed me. It was easy to follow the leading of the Spirit during the process, and after developing a track record of trust. I learned to trust the Spirit throughout the process, even when I couldn't comprehend the end from the beginning. God captured my heart and took time establishing a relationship with me, and eventually, my pursuit for Him became a necessity. I needed His words to confirm me. I needed His presence to fulfill me, and I needed His trust to secure me. During these times, God purified my heart, sanctified my body, and completed an internal work by breaking down the masculinity of my soul. The walls fell, and I learned to submit myself to God and to understand the virtuousness of my identity. I was taught womanhood internally, and it manifested externally.

God began to adorn me and prepare me for Himself. I became a crown in the palm of God's hand. He held me as a jewel in His hand and declared "Daughter no more shall they call you rejected, and your life shall no longer be called ruined, for you shall be called my delight because I delight in you, and your land shall be like a wedding celebration. For even as a young man marries his virgin bride, so shall your builder marry you, and as a bridegroom is happy with his bride, so shall your God be happy with you. Progress Sophia into the woman I ordained you to be."

God reset my life by progressively grooming me to be His bride.

Six

The Backlash

THE BACKLASH WAS REAL. TWO THOUSAND AND EIGHT was one of the most beautiful, yet difficult years of my walk. After God used the Mother's Day prank to transform my exterior, all hell broke out. I was abruptly forced to rediscover my identity and get to know the new Sophia. I felt like a foreigner in a new country and needed help adjusting to this new life. I needed mentors, advocates, and friends to help my journey through the land of new. I was disappointed quickly, as the very ones who began the journey with me, left me hanging to tour this new identity on my own. The things I thought I knew about myself were once again interrupted by God, so I had to spend time learning new things. I was holding on tight to the last thing that kept me secure in my identity as a stud, and that was my appearance. I had no warning, no heads up, and no time to prepare privately for the major transformation. Once again God literally relocated me without warning. If I could describe the range of my emotions, I felt confused, lost, and lonely, yet I was open to embracing the newness because it was all supernatural. I was awestruck and filled with amazement.

The fact that it wasn't planned or rehearsed, and turned out to be a permanent transformation, leaves me speechless at the uniqueness of God's power to perform a miracle, sign and wonder right before my eyes. I know I'm a miracle because I wasn't just dressing like a man, but I was convinced I was a man with female genitals. To strip me of the link that connected me with my manhood, was a powerful God-ordained moment. No man was able to boast or get the glory out of this encounter. This was totally a God ordained encounter of God completing what he began. The moment I crashed into myself in the mirror was the instant the miracles manifested before my eyes. I couldn't deny the power of God, and how He had facilitated such a deliverance. The final chain that had held me bound and tormented me for years was demolished. I was intrigued by the fact that I could no longer fit any of my masculine clothes. It was as if God made everything oversized and so big that I couldn't get into the clothes at all. Everything flopped off of me, and everything was uncomfortable, from the pants to the shoes. I tried to make myself put on my old garments, yet I would feel sick, and God would say, "You've outgrown those clothes, Sophia." God gave me new oil for my new wineskin. I was in awe. I had never witnessed such power, so I yielded and embraced the entire process.

I was thinking, "Finally the people who anticipated this moment would be excited that my debut of femininity has arrived." Instead, I was greeted with snickering, laughing, and sarcastic remarks like, "You look cute girl." Now there were many people who cheered me on and generously applauded what God had completed, but on the other side, the warfare was unbearable. I felt like I was starting over from the beginning because of the demonic attacks that were coming from every side.

Here are some of the barriers I endured post-transformation:

Finding My Style

It took me a while to find my own style, due to everything being new. I had to find Sophia in the process of dressing, so for years I was styled by others until I became conformable with my own niche. I would check out other women, and to my surprise, it wasn't to get with them sexually, but I was sizing them up to observe their styles. I was trying to figure out how I was going to put pieces together to get specific looks. I didn't have much style. I knew what I liked in a woman, yet when it came to styling myself, I wasn't sure what to wear. I was always stylish and materialistic as a stud. I was known for being one of the best dressed in my hood. I rocked everything name brand and matched my shoes with my baseball hats and jackets. Getting dressed came easily for me. So suddenly having to adjust to more feminine attire was difficult. I was used to wearing oversized pants and big shirts that hid my figure, so now seeing my shape and recognizing

I had hips threw me off. I was like, " Yo what am I supposed to do with all this." I could no longer hide my figure, and this was becoming a battle. I quickly knew tight clothes were out of the question, so I had a balanced middle style. No baggy, no skinny, just right fitting clothes were my choice.

I ended up trying multiple styles over the years, and if you look at the history of my progression, my style was all over the place until I learned to embrace my own uniqueness. Even now I am ever learning to embrace my uniqueness, and find Sophia in my style of dress. At the beginning of my process post-transformation, I was wearing Capri pants, flip-flops, shirts with big flowers pinned on them, long skirts and colorful bulky jewelry. Of course over time style changed, and as the seasons shifted, so did my style as I searched to define my new found identity. I learned to embrace my body and became more comfortable picking out clothes that fit. As I found my own edge, dressing became fun. I discovered a sense of style and comfort. I also learned that it wasn't the clothes that made me more feminine. It was my submission and ability to be led into the beauty and wholeness preordained for me.

YIKES I'M INSECURE

One of the characteristics I had as a stud was a strong sense of pride. I was confident, arrogant and cocky. I didn't struggle with many insecurities regarding my appearance. I worked hard on my masculinity and was confident in how I looked. Insecurities were far from me as I felt like I was the baddest stud alive. You couldn't tell me anything.

Once I made the transformation, I began to develop many insecurities based on the newness of my appearance. The darkness and strength of masculinity was broken, so I was trying to adapt to the change, and often times I felt ugly, deformed, and weird. I was doing the best I could to coordinate and put my pieces together perfectly, however, I still didn't have it all together. I had some good and bad days as I looked at myself in the mirror and wondered where Sophia had gone. I would often rub my face, shake myself, and say, "Okay I can wake up now from this nightmare." Every time I felt overwhelmed, God would remind me that the old me was buried, never to be resurrected again. I continued to press forward. I realized that some of my insecurities derived from negative comments made by other people. The same people who couldn't wait to see me in a skirt and prayed me through, were the same ones who poked fun at me, and laughed at my style. I had one woman make a statement that I was fine as a stud, and looked better the way I was. When I tell you that stabbed me to the core, as that was such a relapse statement that could have knocked me back. That statement broke my spirit, but I was determined to keep moving forward and keep my eyes on the prize.

I can recall people making all types of negative comments, and I couldn't understand it. How is it that I was talked about as a stud, and now I'm talked about as a believer. I struggled with the critic's negative statements and found myself becoming more socially isolated. People were mocking and shaming me with their words, and like darts stabbing me in my back, it was painful. Everywhere I turned it was something else negative that I had to deal with. I felt like I couldn't win for losing. I was asked why you wearing that? Why you choose that? Why not this or why not that? With tears in my eyes, I tried to defend myself by saying, "This is what I like." All the while my insides were screaming, "Heck you people are never pleased." I was so ashamed my head would hang down, and I would be paranoid wondering who's saying something and what are they saying. I kept saying, "God this is your doing, why are people trying to intercept my progress?" Yet the entire time God continued to compliment me and encourage me that I was beautiful and wonderfully made. I simply endured the process of dealing with the opinions of others and continued to progress until I became comfortable being uniquely me, and the power of insecurities was broken. There were times insecurities would still try to arise, but I would bind the enemy by reminding him that this is the Lord's doing and it's marvelous.

CAN I ENCOURAGE YOU BEFORE MOVING FORWARD?

Don't you dare quit based on people taunting you and making you feel ashamed of being the man or woman God ordained you to be. Don't relapse in your journey. Don't throw in the towel. Don't yield to the voices of man, instead hear God and know that He is the driver of your life. Hand over the steering wheel and allow Him to dress you. Don't ever abort your progress based on the opinion of man, God is with you.

ALL EYES ON ME

During my lifestyle of living as a homosexual stud, I gathered attention everywhere I went. I would always have someone pointing at me, questioning my gender or being curious. Many homosxuals who are rejected seek the approval and attaention from others. That's why rejected people gravitate to the lifestyle. No matter who, what or where you are, the need for attention is like a force that drives you. I loved the attention; I longed for it and ensured that I received it. However, once I walked through my deliverance and got to the point of post-transformation, I did everything possible to make myself invisible. I didn't want anyone to see me. I hated going out in public because now I was the center of attention, which made me extremely uncomfortable. I developed anxiety, and anytime I was put on the spot, I would sweat and panic until the attention was off of me.

I resided in a very small town where everyone knew everyone. It was literally impossible to hide in a town so small. I mean, my name was ringing in the city, as if I was the president or the pope. People were gossiping, whispering, and discussing my life daily. I was being persecuted on every side. I could be in the mall, the store, or a restaurant, and people would walk up to me screaming, "Oh my God is that you Sophia? Aren't you that gay girl Sophia? Oh, My God, you look like a girl now. Girl, what happened to you? Why'd you change? So you trying to be straight now?" I was taken aback to all these criticisms. I would always think, "who says things like that to someone?" I regularly heard statements like that from several people. I would be so humiliated and ashamed. I just wanted to run away and never look back. I mean this went on for years. I didn't see this as a testimony, I saw it as humiliation. Shame overtook me on every side. I would cry out to God asking, "Why, did you free me; was it to embarrass me? When is this part of my life going to end? How long must I suffer the consequences?" I felt like I was set up. I couldn't understand why so many people were making a big deal out of me turning my life around. When I became overwhelmed, God would always come to my rescue. I was bearing my cross. I refused to quit. I refused to throw in the towel. I was too far to go back. I kept progressing believing that out of this entire process, I would reap a harvest. The power of pride was broken, and humility was my portion as I learned to progress in my femininity.

FALSE PRESSURE

"Now that she look like a girl, she needs a man." After I had begun to become comfortable with my transformation, the next level of pressure came from people pressing me to date. At first, it was put on a skirt or dress like a girl. Now that I was transformed, the pressure of "Girl you need a man" became the next attack. People were questioning and wondering if I was still gay based on me not having a relationship. I was looked at with the side eye and pressured to get into relationships was the new daily conversation with the saints. It was a constant war, and it went from one extreme to the next. I was asked, "Are you dating? Girl who you dating? When are you going to date?" The questions flooded my life like a hurricane. I refused to date for the purpose of covering my shame. I wasn't in need of fig leaves; I needed to be made whole.

The moment I began to feel whole, complete, and secure in my deliverance, the enemy would release a bomb to torment my mind. He would use my singleness to harass me and make me uncomfortable with being single. People would question my deliverance and wonder If I was still gay, and would make accusations along the journey. I was highly supervised and my friendships were suffering attack based on my past. I was trying so hard to learn Sophia. I didn't have space in my life to add a relationship during the most vulnerable phases of my walk. I was still wounded and healing in areas, trying to rediscover my purpose, yet man was attempting to facilitate how my deliverance should play out.

A few years after progressing, when I met a man the first thing I wanted to do was sleep with him to prove to others I was delivered. The enemy attempted to use the shame in my life to produce a counterfeit life by having me leave one lifestyle of sin for another lifestyle of sin. I was advised that God didn't like homosexuality but he would tolerate fornication. I had to continue to overcome the voices of the enemy and believe God for the completion of my story. I overcame the subterfuge of the emeny and continued to progress, refusing to entertain sexual immorality. I just desired to be made whole. Heterosexuality is not the cure for homosexuality, deliverance is.

Tried and Tested

God amazes me on how He journeyed me through deliverance and used humor to transform my life. There were times I was tempted to engage in same-sex encounters, and the power of God would interfere. My sex drive and desire for intimacy with a woman no longer made sense in my head. The very thing that connected me to my sexuality was my masculinity, and now that God had taken away my manhood, I was rendered helpless. I couldn't make the connection of being sexually active with a woman without being the man. The spirit of deception is strong, and the delusion is real. My sexuality was connected to my ability to imagine and use illusion to create the sexual atmosphere needed to perform. The renewal of my mind, transformed, I began to see myself in a different light. Every time I tried to conjure up an imagination, I would draw blanks.

I began to see women in a different way and learned to enjoy women without lusting after them sexually. However, there were times in my journey where the enemy would entice me with my past and use attractions to lure me into darkness. At this point post-transformation, I had developed the legal authority to resist the enemy. At the beginning of my walk, I spent years trying to rebuke the devil, yet I had no power. I learned the secret of getting rid of the enemy, and that was by taking on the role of submission. I had to learn to submit to God, which empowered me to resist the devil so that he would flee. I learned to cast down the imaginations when they occurred, and I used spiritual warfare to maintain my deliverance. There were moments of cravings and desires, yet my appetite for God became greater than my appetite for lust.

The idea of being seven times worse than I was before salvation caused me to fear to return to the vomit I had been delivered from. The temptations were real, and the backlash was assigned to create situations to lure me back, but when God delivered me, He became my strong tower to run into for safety. The temptations were realer than ever before, as the enemy upgraded the darts by brining women and men I could only dream of dating. I was being hit with double whammies as I found myself being taunted. As I had strength to turn down women, men were standing at the gate of perversion with a devouring appetite to introduce me to a realm that's been unknown. Perversion was at an all time high as sexual invitations were knocking on the door like kids playing ding-dong ditch. I wanted purity more than perversion, so I had to learn to flee immorality, which wasn't easy, but it was worth it.

The spirit of homosexuality lost its grip when I discovered the beauty of being a woman. I learned the value and purpose of my womanhood, and that it wasn't to be delivered just from sex, but to be a representative of the bride of Christ in the earth. I learned the value of my temple, and that it was no longer under my authority, but owned by the Holy Spirit.

Seven

THE VICTORY
(Victory Belongs to Jesus)

I HAD TO LEARN THAT VICTORY BELONGS TO JESUS. Although the enemy had attempted to stand against the Lord, he's a defeated foe. The moment I accepted Jesus Christ as my personal Savior, the victory was in Him. His blood handled my sin, and although I walked out this lifestyle progressively, it was by His grace. The enemy tried to use my process as a stumbling block, making me believe the victory was in me, yet the battle was won on the cross. I put my lifestyle on the shoulders of Jesus and trusted that He would allow me to pass through gracefully. I credit Jesus for using my process, to know, learn, discover, and appreciate His death, burial, and resurrection. I found the love of the Father through the journey and developed a personal relationship with the Holy Spirit; which was Truth in my life. The process was never about me winning battles; it was about me discovering a deeper level of the Father along the way.

As I walked out my deliverance, I began to embrace who God ordained me to be. The scales on my eyes were removed, and I began to see myself through the blood. Jesus got inside the boat of my life, and showed me how to reposition my net until I broke through in every area of my life. Throughout this entire journey, I went from glory to glory, learning God in multiple facets. The anointing of Jesus destroyed every yoke in my life, and demonstrated that there is nothing too hard for Him.

It's important that you trust God with your entire life and stand on Jeremiah 29:11. It is the heart of God to give you a hope and a future, and bring you to an expected end. The enemy may show you where you are, but God sees where you are going. Now relax, take a deep breath and praise God for sealing the deal of your deliverance on the cross. You are already liberated, now soar! The backlash will occur due to the fact that you are impacting the Kingdom while terrorizing hell. The enemy knows that you are his opponent, and are no longer on his team, so he releases vicious attacks to counter your breakthrough. Remember God isn't just coming to deliver you from sex, but He is dismantling the very system that's been holding you bound. The very culture in which the enemy has tried to keep you has been destroyed, that you may go forth and pronounce freedom to the captives.

Eight

∞

EXHORTATION

I DON'T KNOW WHO YOU ARE, READING THIS BOOK right now, but I want to encourage you that victory belongs to Jesus. You may feel stuck, bound, and engulfed in sin, and unsure of what's next. It is in Jesus that you are free, liberated, and able to defeat the enemy in your life. The blood has already set you free. You are not in a battle fighting for the victory; you are in the battle discovering grace, compassion, and the love of the Father on a greater level. The enemy is aware that he's a defeated foe, and he's attempting to rob you of your peace, praise, and worship. This battle is not yours; it belongs to the Lord. As you praise God in the process, He will set an ambush around your enemies. Don't you dare question your deliverance! If you accepted Christ as your personal savior, you are free! Whom the son sets free is free indeed. Walk through your journey and find joy in the process. God is going to use your story. You are being trained to be the "comeback kid" for someone else. You are the bloodline breaker and shall be used in the days to come. Remember the victory is in Jesus.

Parents

Parents, don't you dare give up on your child! You are the very voice they need to confirm and reaffirm them. I know your child may look bound and may very well be bound in homosexuality, but there is nothing too hard for God. Stop allowing the enemy to terrorize you by trying to have you reject the seed you were anointed to protect. I know your heart is bleeding and you can't figure out why your child, but why not your child? Your child is a comeback kid and will be one who will disrupt darkness for their generation. God works in mysterious ways, and the moment you think it's over, God has already made a way of escape. I prophesy that your child is coming home, and will be used to bankrupt the systems of perversion that has them bound. You may not be able to see what God is doing, but go up in the spirit, and release a shout of victory for it's already done. Reverse word curses spoken over their life, and command the spirit of rejection, abandonment, deception and trauma to be uprooted. Cancel the assignment of the enemy off of their lives now. Don't call them by the sin that you see, call them by name and remind God that they belong to Him.

Remind God that before He formed them in your womb, He had a plan and purpose for their lives that can't be altered or reversed. Command that the gates of hell shall not prevail against your bloodline. Arise mothers and prophesy! Arise fathers and prophesy! Don't settle for it's over, it's too late, and there is nothing else you can do. You have something you can do, praise and prophesy!

Even as God supernaturally delivered me, so shall your seed be delivered. I prophesy that because you have this book in your presence, whoever you know that's bound, shall be set free! I speak to the four winds of the earth and command winds of deliverance to blow upon your child now! I declare testimonies shall arise, and your child shall return unto you with double honor thanking you for not giving up on them.

I speak to the parent who has already cut their child off because of their lifestyle that your relationship will be restored. I speak restoration now. May broken hearts be mended, may unforgiveness be broken, and forgiveness released. May the power of God use your love, mom or dad, to propel your child to return.

It may look like when you pray things are getting worse, but know that things get worse before they get better. Set your gaze on God who is the author and finisher of your faith. Know that God will complete the work, and your child will be used to impact the kingdom. Take rest in God and know that when you prayed the first time, you were heard, and all of heaven is responding. Rejoice, and celebrate. Prepare the party for your prodigal is returning and when they return you won't intervene and abort the process. God got this!

LEADERS

Leaders, catch the fish. Get in the boat, and help the sons and daughters you are praying for reposition their nets until they get a breakthrough. Establish relationship, find out the strongman, and de-route it. Demonstrate the love of the

Father, and be the light that breaks through the darkness. Don't interrupt or use your formula to perform deliverance, but allow God to drive demons out little by little, as you remain on standby, being used as God instructs you. Don't try to operate with human intellect, be sensitive to the spirit, and handle souls with care. Discern the process of those you are assigned to shepherd and oversee. Don't treat every case the same, use your wisdom to deliver for the Deliverer has already delivered. Use your anointing to demonstrate love which covers a multitude of sin.

It may be hard and appear to be a trend, but this adversary is real and has released this demonic attack upon the youth and young adults like never before. Preach with fire, compassion, and conviction until the truth sets them free. Allow the word to pierce the hearts until the power of God is manifested. Be like Jesus, spend time establishing a relationship until you are able to gain ground and bind the strongman. Once you have gained access and have swept the house, fill it with the Word and love of God.

Leaders don't allow the spirit of homosexuality to intimidate you and keep you from speaking truth, yet do it in love, and do in under the guidance of the Holy Spirit. Don't use your platform to kill the soul who's already wounded. Don't judge a book by its cover. Just because the person is bound to residue doesn't mean they are not striving for holiness. Use wisdom and ask God to reveal the heart of those assigned to you. Don't be discouraged, you have been equipped, and trained to work with hard cases, and once you walk sons and daughters out of darkness into light, you will be remembered and blessed all the days of your life. Remember the comeback kids and rookies are arising, and the one you are praying for just may be the one.

You

You're not reading this book by coincidence. This is for you, and to encourage you that you are not by yourself. You were born to accomplish great things in the earth, and even as the enemy has appeared to be winning, he's defeated. You are free, God loves you, and He will never leave you or forsake you. God has plans to use your life now and in the days to come. You may not know why God chose you, but before the foundation of the world, your days were accounted for. God did not make a mistake with you, He created you in His image and after His likeness. You are getting your identity back today. You were born on purpose with a purpose the enemy has been stealing from you since the birth canal because he's aware of your assignment in the earth. He knows you are chosen to break his plots and plans, and that you are called to be the bloodline breaker for your bloodline.

Don't you dare abort your process or throw in the towel because it's too difficult. Remember God is with you, and it's not by might, nor by power but by the spirit. Let go of the steering wheel of your life and allow God to drive. Stop fighting and surrender, for He has need of you. Embrace your journey and walk this transformation out. Allow God to strip you of the very residue that's granting the enemy access. Trust God to complete the entire process, and lean not on your own understanding. You're at the finish line; you can do this! Soon you will be the blueprint for others by telling them your story. You are a comeback kid, now arise, remove your grave clothes, and embrace the new life God has set aside and ordained for you.

Allow my story and journey to encourage you that God is there the entire time. It is my prayer that this book has stirred you, blessed you, and encouraged you. No matter what you are bound by, God is a deliverer. You may look or feel like God isn't moving or responding to your prayers, but God's timing is not your time. He works all things decently and in order. He knows the plans He has for you, and His ways are not your ways, nor are His thoughts, your thoughts. If God began a good work in you, He will complete it. This book demonstrates how God delivered me little by little and restored my life one thousand fold.

The enemy must repay you and your bloodline for his deadly attack. God is not just going to deliver you for your own selfish gain. He's going to use your life to destroy the curse on the bloodline. Many people see my platform and who I am today, yet they have no idea of the number of death decrees I survived. I am a comeback kid, and God has reset my life. He has given me beauty for ashes, and double honor for my shame. Allowing Jesus to take the wheel in my life has opened up doors beyond my imagination. You may be looking at your life today, hating the process you are in, but I am here to prophesy that it will not be like this always. God is progressing you for your next level. Now arise and shine and know that your light has come, and the glory of the Lord has risen upon you. I prophesy that your identity is being reset and that you shall be who you were ordained to be before the foundation of the world. I declare that the grip of deception is broken, and the truth of who you are is released. I break every contract of "I'll never" off of your life, and release the word of the Lord upon you. You are Chosen, now Arise and be Unapologetically Dope. You won't die in your process, and the very culture of homosexuality is dismantled. You just relocated in the spirit realm.

This is not the closing, but the beginning for you to go deeper, seek greater and engage further. Today we walk into the formation of progression. Today I prophesy that you will become exactly who God has ordained you to be. Your language, your posture, and your position shall progress to another level. Behind the shell of your outer exterior, there is a very beautiful being waiting to be released. You are not your lifestyle, you are not your sexuality, you are God's seed, and the seed that's in you shall manifest and be revealed. Your posture has shifted from a place of defeat to a place of victory. Progression gives God the opportunity to take you from glory to glory, a consistent advancement; therefore advance Into the life that's been pre-ordained just for you. I declare that a series of victories will break out upon your life. You may feel like you're in last place, but the last shall finish first.

A cycle of success shall be your portion. Your adversity has set you up for the greatest outpouring of your life. I love you, and I am waiting on you for the kingdom has need of you. *Arise Comeback kid, Arise!*

About the Publisher

Let us bring your story to life! With Life to Legacy, we offer the following publishing services: manuscript development, editing, transcription services, ghostwriting, cover design, copyright services, ISBN assignment, worldwide distribution, and eBook production and distribution.

Throughout the entire production process, you maintain control over your project. We also specialize in family history books, so you can leave a written legacy for your children, grandchildren, and others. You put your story in our hands, and we'll bring it to literary life! We have several publishing packages to meet all your publishing needs.

Call us at: 877-267-7477, or you can also send e-mail to: Life2Legacybooks@att.net. Please visit our Web site:

www.Life2Legacy.com

www.ingramcontent.com/pod-product-compliance
Lightning Source LLC
Chambersburg PA
CBHW030944090426
42737CB00007B/532